Separation and Divorce

ISSUES
(formerly Issues for the Nineties)

Volume 40

Editor

Craig Donnellan

First published by Independence
PO Box 295
Cambridge CB1 3XP
England

© Craig Donnellan 1999

British Library Cataloguing in Publication Data
Separation and Divorce – (Issues Series)
I. Donnellan, Craig II. Series
306.8'9

ISBN 1 86168 082 1

Printed in Great Britain
City Print Ltd
Milton Keynes

Typeset by
Claire Boyd

Cover
The illustration on the front cover is by
Pumpkin House.

CONTENTS

Chapter One: When Marriage Breaks Down

Marriage in crisis	*1*
A short guide to divorce in England and Wales	*2*
Divorce 'does not damage most children'	*4*
The impact on children and adolescents	*5*
When parents split up	*7*
The Children (Scotland) Act 1995 and you	*8*
What will happen to me if my parents split up or divorce?	*9*
What happens to me when my parents split up?	*10*
Record 5.3 million people live alone	*11*
Dilemma	*12*
Let children veto divorce, suggests Left-wing report	*14*
Married parents, a child's best start in life	*15*
Forget the family says charity . . . we have networks	*16*
Pre-marriage pacts 'a peril' say churchmen	*17*
A better way	*18*
Next generation	*20*
Endless love?	*21*
Family life	*22*
Divorcees' pensions 'could hit marriage'	*23*
The sad fall-out when families split	*24*
Wives 'less happy with married life than men'	*26*
Labour backs prenuptial deals	*26*
15,000 wedding awaydays	*27*
Britons delaying nuptial rights as costs top £10,000	*27*

Chapter Two: Seeking Help

Separating or divorcing?	*28*
UK College of Family Mediators	*29*
The good divorce guide	*30*
The secret of a happy divorce	*34*
The Family Court Service	*35*
Welcome to Relate	*36*
Family mediation	*37*
Getting a divorce	*38*
Additional resources	*41*
Index	*42*
Web site information	*43*
Acknowledgements	*44*

Introduction

Separation and Divorce is the fortieth volume in the series: **Issues**. The aim of this series is to offer up-to-date information about important issues in our world.

Separation and Divorce looks at recent trends and ways of dealing with marriage breakdowns.

The information comes from a wide variety of sources and includes:
Government reports and statistics
Newspaper reports and features
Magazine articles and surveys
Literature from lobby groups
and charitable organisations.

It is hoped that, as you read about the many aspects of the issues explored in this book, you will critically evaluate the information presented. It is important that you decide whether you are being presented with facts or opinions. Does the writer give a biased or an unbiased report? If an opinion is being expressed, do you agree with the writer?

Separation and Divorce offers a useful starting-point for those who need convenient access to information about the many issues involved. However, it is only a starting-point. At the back of the book is a list of organisations which you may want to contact for further information.

*****

CHAPTER ONE: WHEN MARRIAGE BREAKS DOWN

Marriage in crisis

By Helen Carroll

The *Mail* has conducted the most comprehensive study ever into the state of modern marriage. And one of the most surprising findings is that almost twice as many unmarried men than women want to marry in the future – 61 per cent compared with 37 per cent.

This goes against the traditional assumption that it is women who always want to rush down the aisle while men are the ones who are terrified of commitment.

So how can we explain this statistic uncovered by pollsters Mori in face-to-face interviews with 2,000 people?

A proportion of these women will be those who have been through one divorce and don't want to risk another.

Many are career women who are increasingly refusing to play the role of the traditional wife, who does the housework and looks after the children as well as holding down a job.

Others will be women who are discovering that no human being can give them everything they have been told to expect by women's glossy magazines, which have raised expectations out of all reality.

Another fascinating finding is that fidelity in marriage is deemed more important by the young than the middle-aged. Among 25 to 34-year-olds, 78 per cent believe it is wrong to have an extra-marital affair, compared with 69 per cent of 45 to 54-year-olds. It is the younger generation, as the first to suffer the fall-out from rising divorce figures, who are leading the backlash against the permissive society that has prevailed in Britain since the Sixties. Sarah Blower of relationship counselling service Relate says: 'There is evidence of a shift in the value placed on commitment in our society. Marriage is a positive way of expressing commitment, and that is

why young people are moving back towards it. People are beginning to value other caring, sharing ways of leading their lives within a family unit.

'At the same time people have been forced to take notice of increasing evidence showing that children of divorced parents suffer in a way that can often affect their emotional development and performance at school. Parents experiencing problems are more likely to be encouraged to sort out their differences but stay together for the sake of the children.' However, it is the same young people who value fidelity in marriage who confess to promiscuity before committing to one partner. One-fifth of 25 to 34-year-olds have had more than ten sexual partners.

How can this be reconciled with their greater belief in faithfulness in marriage? Perhaps these figures suggest the younger age group is determined to 'try out' potential partners before committing to marriage. The dramatic fall in the numbers who value church over register office weddings indicates that the change in attitude towards marriage is not governed by religious beliefs but more likely to be a reaction against social ills, including crime and benefit dependency, which are a result of family break-ups and single motherhood.

Nearly half the population believe there should be legislation to make it harder to divorce, while more than one-third think tougher tests should be used to assess a couple's suitability for marriage. This, they believe, would go some way towards halting the growing trend towards single-parent families in Britain.

- A representative national sample of 2,000 adults took part in face-to-face interviews for the poll conducted by researchers Mori in October last year.

- Infidelity is the reason nearly a third of marriages fall apart.
- Three-quarters of people believe in marriage, while 64 per cent say marriage should be for ever.
- Among unmarried under-45s, more than two-thirds want to wed in the future.
- 61 per cent of unmarried men want to tie the knot, compared with just 37 per cent of single women.
- One-fifth of those in the 25 to 34-year-old age bracket have had more than ten sexual partners.
- 81 per cent believe it is wrong to have an extra-marital affair – 4 per cent more than in 1991.
- Among under-25s, 70 per cent believe it important to live with a partner before marrying, while 53 per cent of under-45s who are married have cohabited.
- 67 per cent of under-45s believe it is acceptable to have a child outside wedlock.
- More than one-fifth of people believe in the importance of pre-nuptial agreements.
- Only 28 per cent believe it is better to marry in a church than a register office.

The most important reasons for divorce

A representative national sample of 2,000 adults took part in face-to-face interviews for the poll conducted by researchers Mori in October last year.

Reason	%
Career pressure on man	1%
Boredom	1%
In-laws/family problems	2%
Lack of respect for each other	2%
Lack of money/financial problems	2%
Alcohol	3%
Violence	8%
Don't know	9%
Growing apart	18%
Unreasonable behaviour	23%
Unfaithfulness	31%

Source: MORI

Reasons why we divorce

- Unfaithfulness 31 per cent
- Growing apart 19 per cent
- Unreasonable behaviour 16 per cent
- Violence 5 per cent
- Alcohol 4 per cent
- Lack of money 2 per cent
- Lack of respect for each other 2 per cent
- Boredom 2 per cent
- In-laws/family problems 2 per cent
- Career pressures on men 2 per cent

© *The Daily Mail January, 1998*

A short guide to divorce in England and Wales

Introduction

The mechanics of obtaining a divorce nowadays are usually quite straightforward, particularly if the couple agree that the marriage is over. The difficulties tend to lie rather with related issues such as money matters and arrangements for children.

The purpose of this short guide is to outline the divorce process itself so that you may see what is involved. It does not cover defended divorces, disputes concerning children or financial issues. You should consult a solicitor for any of that. It is not meant to be a comprehensive or stand-alone analysis of the law and it should not be used in that way. It will help you to see what is involved in getting divorced.

By Steve Austin

The jargon

The person who starts the divorce is called 'the Petitioner'. The other person is 'the Respondent'.

The grounds for divorce

You must have grounds to start a divorce. If you are going to start a divorce then you must show that the marriage has irretrievably broken down and that:

1. Your spouse has committed adultery and you find it intolerable to live with them; or
2. Your spouse has behaved in such a way that you cannot reasonably be expected to live with them; or
3. Your spouse has deserted you for a continuous period of at least 2 years; or
4. You and your spouse have lived apart for a continuous period of at least 2 years and your spouse consents to a divorce; or
5. You and your spouse have lived apart for a continuous period of at least 5 years.

You must have been married for over a year in order to start a divorce.

It does not matter where you were married, but one of you must either be domiciled in England and Wales or have been resident there for the last year.

Myths exploded

Divorcing on the basis of separation is generally no quicker than on any other basis. In the vast majority of cases, there is no financial advantage to being the Petitioner (the one star{9ng the divorce). Apart from in very extreme circumstances, you will have the same rights to money, maintenance and property whether you are the Petitioner or the Respondent. The main exception to this is the fact that if you are the Petitioner, you can try to claim from the other person the legal costs of the divorce.

The costs that can be claimed are the costs of getting the divorce and not the costs of sorting out any other matters, such as financial disputes. On average, the costs, if you instruct a solicitor, are usually five hundred pounds or so and it may not be worth pursuing such a claim.

If you are divorcing on the basis of adultery, you can name on the divorce papers the other person concerned. This, again, does not usually give you any financial advantage and it can sometimes have the effect of slowing down the divorce process. We usually recommend that you do not name anyone else.

The divorce petition

This is the document that starts the divorce. It contains the information which is required by the court and sets out the basis of the divorce. It finishes by asking the court to dissolve the marriage. It also contains a section including all the possible financial claims which the Petitioner has (even if it is not really intended to pursue them).

It is often sensible to try to obtain the other person's consent to the petition before starting the divorce.

Starting the divorce

The divorce petition (and a statement setting out the arrangements for the children if there are children) is sent to the court with the marriage certificate (and some other bits and pieces). The court opens a file for the papers and sends the divorce petition out in the post to the Respondent.

Divorce proceedings are usually held in private. The chances are that you will not have to attend court in relation to your divorce (unless there are disputes over money matters or the arrangements for the children), but if you do have to attend, the public and the press will not normally be allowed into your courtroom. The press rarely publish any details of divorces but they are allowed to publish the fact that a divorce has been granted.

The acknowledgement of service form

At the same time as sending out the divorce petition, the court also sends to the Respondent a questionnaire called 'the acknowledgement of service form'. The Respondent fills it in to say that they have received the divorce papers and (hopefully) that they do not intend to defend the divorce. Most divorces are undefended. In the case of a divorce based on allegations of unreasonable behaviour, it is usually quite all right for the Respondent to say that the allegations are not admitted but that the divorce will be undefended. (Check with your solicitor for a proper understanding of how this works.)

The Respondent returns the form to the court and the court sends it to the Petitioner or his/her solicitors.

The next step

The Petitioner then has to ask the court to progress the divorce. This is done by sending to the court a 'sworn' statement (called an 'affidavit') which, in brief, confirms that the content of the divorce petition is correct and that the Petitioner wishes to go ahead with the divorce. The Petitioner has to swear on the Bible (alternatives are available if the Petitioner has religious objections) in front of an independent solicitor or court official that the statement is true.

Decree nisi

Once the statement has been sent to the court, the judge will look at all of the papers. If he believes that everything is in order, he will set a date for the pronouncement of the 'decree nisi' of divorce. The court will send out a piece of paper saying when the decree nisi will be formally pronounced. There is not usually any need to attend court on the day that the decree nisi is pronounced (unless there is any dispute about whether or not the Respondent should pay the costs of the divorce).

A short while after the pronouncement of the decree nisi, the court office will type the decree nisi document and post it to the parties.

The decree nisi does not mean that the divorce is final. It is simply a confirmation that the court is satisfied that the divorce may proceed.

Decree absolute

In order to make the divorce final, the Petitioner must apply to the court for 'decree absolute'. The Petitioner sends to the court a simple form asking for the decree absolute. The Petitioner is not allowed to do this until 6 weeks and a day have gone by since the date of the decree nisi. The court will process the form, and the judge will pronounce decree absolute. Shortly afterwards, the court office will type up the decree absolute document and send it out to the parties.

If the Petitioner does not apply for decree absolute, then the Respondent can do so but must wait a longer time. If the Respondent applies, then there has to be a short court hearing. The pronouncement of decree absolute marks the end of the marriage.

© *Warner Goodman & Streat*

Divorce 'does not damage most children'

By Glenda Cooper, Social Affairs Correspondent

Children whose parents divorce may shows signs of unhappiness in the short term but the majority grow up unscathed with only a small minority suffering long-term problems, a report has found.

With fighting between parents, rather than separation itself, providing most of the problems, the report says society should concentrate on support for the family rather than the institution of marriage itself as divorce rates continue to rise inexorably.

But charities and campaigning groups attacked the controversial study, published b the Joseph Rowntree Foundation, saying previous studies had shown that parents' separation can scar children for years and that the full problems caused by divorce might not yet be known.

The major review of more than 200 British research studies, spanning more than 30 years, has concluded that while for a couple of years children may have difficulties such as bed-wetting, bad behaviour and low self-esteem, most children grow out of this and develop normally.

It also challenges some widely-held views on divorce, saying that the age at which children experience separation is not important, there is no consistent evidence to show boys are more badly affected than girls, and absence of a parent figure is not the most influential feature of separation on a child's development.

More than half of couples who divorce have children under 16, and if recent trends continue, one in five children born to married couples will experience parental divorce by the age of 16. However, these figures may underestimate the true rate of family dissolution as they do not include the separation of cohabiting couples.

As the immediate distress starts to fade, most children settle down and develop normally. 'Most children are fine after a short period,' said Dr Jan Pryor, from the University of Auckland and one of the authors of the report. In a small minority, however, there is a greater probability of poor out comes which reach into adult life – and these are often twice as common as they are among children whose parents have stayed together.

More than half of couples who divorce have children under 16

Factors which put children of separated families at increased risk include those who live in poor households, leave school without qualifications, leave home while young and have children as a teenager.

Family conflict, whether before, during or after separation, is particularly stressful for children who may respond by becoming anxious, aggressive or withdrawn. 'Children find conflict difficult and distressing,' said Dr Pryor. 'Our message to parents is to keep children away from it. Children can observe conflict and be drawn down into it. One of the most damaging things is when parents use children as go-betweens. We would say avoid that kind of conflict.'

Julia Cole of Relate said that children could recover from divorce if it was settled amicably and if parents continued to act with sympathy and understanding. 'But that's an awful lot of ifs,' she added.

'Conflictual divorce or separation can cause tremendous damage where parents argue or use children as pawns in their games. There is considerable evidence to show children of divorced parents do less well at school and are more likely to get into trouble with the police or grow up and become divorcees themselves,' Ms Cole added.

Jonathan Bartley, general secretary for the Movement for Christian Democracy, said: 'The report underlines that marriage is the key to family life and divorce is a far bigger problem than was previously thought. More liberal attitudes have said that divorce is benign, but

that is clearly not the case. And we still don't know the long-term implications of divorce.'

The report concludes that children and parents should have access to professional support at the time of separation. Help for parents coping with distress will make it easier for them to help their children. GPs, teachers and solicitors should be offered information and training to make it easier for them to advise families or guide them towards more specialist help.

Dr Bryan Rodgers of the Australian National University, Canberra, said: 'One of the messages is that if children are to be protected against the kind of disadvantages identified by research, then they and their parents will need better information and support before, during and after separation.'

The cost of a broken home

Studies on divorce and children over the past three decades have seen a range of differing views:

- In 1993, the National Child Development Study of 11,000 children born in 1958 concluded that children who lost a parent through death did not under-perform in the same way as children of divorce.
- In 1994 an Exeter University study of 152 children found children from broken families had worse health, suffered psychological problems, were more likely to need extra school help at school, had more trouble socialising and suffered low self-esteem.
- In April 1997 a Queen's University of Belfast study of 37 children said marriage breakdown took a heavy toll on the physical and

emotional well-being of teenagers because of the stresses of changing house, school and domestic arrangements.

- In October 1997, a British Psychological Society study of 400 children in South Wales said family break-up turns teenage boys towards aggression, delinquency and crime. The report said teenage boys had more trouble coming to terms with divorce or separation.
- Later in 1998, a combined study of more than 15,000 children born between 1945-70 whose parents separated found that they suffered an educational disadvantage, were more likely to attend special schools and had problems with schoolwork.

© *The Independent*
June, 1998

The impact on children and adolescents

D ivorce affects 150,000 children each year in the UK. If divorce of married parents and separation of unmarried parents are taken into account, nearly half of all children in the UK will face this crisis by the end of their childhoods.

How are children affected?

The child may suffer in his or her own right. There may be the distress and trauma of events leading up to the family break-up, the way the break-up happened and an enormous sense of loss. The child's or adolescent's world may seem turned upside down and he or she may come to feel abnormal and even despairing. It may feel as if they are being rejected or are the cause of the separation.

Many childhood emotional and behavioural problems occur more frequently in situations of marital discord and breakdown. The parting of parents may make the child very insecure and give rise to fears that the remaining parent may also

For parents and teachers

abandon him or her. 'Babyish' behaviour (e.g. bedwetting, 'clinginess', nightmares, worries or naughtiness) may be caused by the separation and occur before or after visits to the non-resident parent. Teenagers may show distress by 'acting out' or becoming withdrawn. Concentration at school may be affected.

The child's trauma may be greatly increased if the warring parents involve the child in their conflict. Children and adolescents can be caught up in the conflict in the following ways:

- One parent's endless criticisms and hostilities about the other.

Many childhood emotional and behavioural problems occur more frequently in situations of marital discord and breakdown

---

- Being asked to take sides, e.g. by being asked with whom they prefer to live, or to produce evidence of fault in a parent.
- A parent appearing helpless and seeing the child's or adolescent's support.

What are the consequences?

Firstly, there are the problems resulting directly from the impact on the child or adolescent of his or her parents no longer loving each other and no longer living together. Examples of these are:

- a sense of loss
- feeling abnormal, with an abnormal family
- a fear of abandonment
- anger at one or both parents for the split-up
- self-blame and guilt about the split-up
- a sense of rejection
- longing for a return to normality, with both parents living together.

Some children, when the marriage or partnership has been very hostile or violent, may be relieved or have mixed feelings when it finally ends.

Secondly, there are the problems resulting from the child or adolescent being brought into the adult squabbles and distress. Children or adolescents may, for example:

- become the focus of the dispute, e.g. money, residence, contact
- come to believe they are to blame for the dispute
- feel torn in two because loyalty to one parent may be seen as betrayal by the other
- feel he or she is not allowed to love both parents or be loved by both parents
- blame one parent for the split-up. Sometimes the child or adolescent identifies with the parent at fault
- be used as a weapon by one parent or the other. Parents may wittingly or unwittingly encourage disturbed behaviour for this purpose.
- live with a parent who is so consumed with anger or distress that there is no one offering the child much parenting or support.

What should be done to help

The aim of any two parents who are splitting up must be to ensure an ongoing relationship with his or her partner for dealing with parenting issues. The golden rule is that the adults (in this case, the parents) must take on the responsibility for what is happening as theirs and theirs alone, and convey this clearly to the young person. Parents must see their role as protecting their children from adult matters and adult responsibilities.

Parents need to be sensitive to how each child may be affected, and how he or she may be feeling and reacting. It is important that parents consider ways of minimising the trauma for the child (making sure he or she feels safe, secure and confident; that problems can be sorted out; and ongoing relationships with each parent sustained). Parents need to look at and discuss between themselves how issues between them may be affecting the child, and how they can protect the child.

The principles guiding parents should be:

- Openness and lots of communication so that the child not only knows what is going on, but feels it is okay to ask questions.
- Reassurance that he or she is still loved by both parents and will be cared for.
- Parents making time to be easily available to the child.
- Reassurance about the future.
- Conveying clearly that while the parents are interested in the child's views, it is they who are responsible for decisions.
- Continuing usual activities and routines, for example seeing friends and members of the extended family, and making as few changes as possible. This helps the child feel life can be normal, and provides support for the child.

How to get help

If there are major difficulties in helping the children cope, it is the parents who need to address these and, if necessary, seek outside help. Your GP will be able to offer support and advice, and to refer on as appropriate. Some children may need specialist help from the local Child and Adolescent Mental Health Service.

Sources of further information

The Children's Society (1988) *Focus on Families: Divorce and its Effects on Children.*
Wells, R. (1989) *Helping Children Cope with Divorce.* Sheldon Press.
Burrett, J. (1993) *To and Fro Children: A Guide to Successful Parenting after Divorce.* Thorsow.

© *Royal College of Psychiatrists*
August, 1998

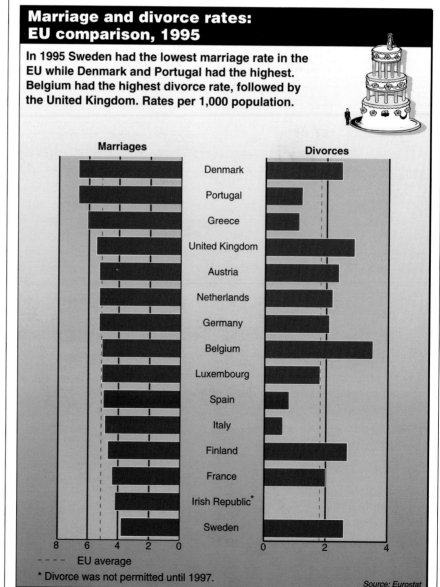

Marriage and divorce rates: EU comparison, 1995

In 1995 Sweden had the lowest marriage rate in the EU while Denmark and Portugal had the highest. Belgium had the highest divorce rate, followed by the United Kingdom. Rates per 1,000 population.

Marriages / Divorces

Denmark
Portugal
Greece
United Kingdom
Austria
Netherlands
Germany
Belgium
Luxembourg
Spain
Italy
Finland
France
Irish Republic*
Sweden

- - - - EU average
* Divorce was not permitted until 1997.

Source: Eurostat

When parents split up

Facts and figures

Do you know that:
- one marriage in three is likely to end in divorce (one in four in Scotland).
- half of all divorces involve children under 16.
- every year 150,000 children in England and Wales (and 9,000 in Scotland) see their parents divorce.
- 33% of these children are under five years old (22% in Scotland).
- 85% to 90% live with their mothers, 10% to 15% with their fathers.
- one child in four will have divorced parents by the age of sixteen.
- the highest number of divorces is after four years of marriage (six years in Scotland); the risk then steadily decreases with the length of marriage.
- one divorce in four is the second divorce for at least one partner (one in ten in Scotland).

The only study of a cross-section of divorced families was in Scotland, in which custodial parents and adolescent children were interviewed (*Children in the Middle* by Ann Mitchell, Tavistock Publications, 1985). This research showed that:
- one-third of the children had lost touch with one parent as an immediate result of the separation; five years after divorce, two-thirds had lost touch.
- subsequent relationships with their non-custodial parents were directly related to speed of arranging access.
- most children would have preferred their parents to stick together, whatever the domestic situation.
- when their parents split up, most children longed to continue a loving relationship with each of them.
- most parents gave their children too little information (or none) about what was happening.
- many children were more aware of their parents' feelings than their parents were of the children's feelings.
- children were more likely to accept a step-parent if they had a good relationship with the non-custodial parent.

Practical effects
After separation, children are likely to:
- live in poorer quality housing.
- have a lower standard of living.
- receive less parental care.
- receive more substitute care (especially the under-fives).
- be latchkey children.
- take on more domestic responsibilities.
- grow up a little faster.

Possibly there will be:
- several changes of home or school.
- changes of main carer.
- a step-parent (married or cohabiting).
- different surnames within the family.

In some families:
- brothers and sisters will be divided between parents (or other relatives).
- children will acquire step-brothers or sisters or half-brothers or sisters.

Emotional effects
Children are likely to:
- be distressed, confused or angry.
- be concerned for their parent(s).
- lose touch with one parent.
- feel rejected by one parent.
- wish for parental reconciliation, even after parental violence and even after remarriage.

Possibly children will:
- not realise separation is final.
- regress in behaviour (especially under-fives).
- blame themselves (especially under-eights).
- feel divided loyalties between their parents.
- lose touch with one set of grandparents.
- be embarrassed, hiding the separation from friends.
- hide their feelings from their parents.
- become aggressive, or delinquent.
- truant.
- need professional help.

At school, children might:
- lose the ability to concentrate; daydream.
- suffer a deterioration in work standards.
- fail to produce their homework.
- be tense, anxious, disobedient, depressed.
- behave worse or better than usual.
- feel the need for someone in whom to confide.

• The above is an extract from *When Parents Split Up*, a pack produced by Family Mediation Scotland. See page 41 for address details.

© Family Mediation Scotland

The Children (Scotland) Act 1995 and you

A guide for young people

What is The Children (Scotland) Act?

The Children (Scotland) Act is an important new law for children and young people. It started on 19th July 1995. It is about how children should be brought up and cared for.

What does the Act say?

It says that:

- When a court is making a decision about a child, their first thought must be what is best for the child.
- A court must put children first when making decisions.
- A court must listen to the child in court cases that are about that child.

Why is the Act important for you?

It gives you certain rights and says that you must be treated with respect. This means:

- You have the right to be listened to.
- You have the right to have your voice heard in court cases that are about you.
- You have the right to your own lawyer and to tell him or her what you want to happen if you are able to understand what is involved.

Family separation

The Act talks about children whose parents are separating or divorcing. If parents cannot agree about your future between them there is a range of orders the court can make that could affect you:

- A *Residence Order* – says where you should live and with whom. Usually you will live with one parent, but the court can make the order in favour of more than one person and say how much time you should spend living with each.
- A *Contact Order* – says who you can visit or stay with overnight or who can visit you or can write to you or who you can talk to on the telephone.
- A *Specific Issue Order* – lets the court decide about something which you and /your parents cannot agree about, for example, matters relating to your health or which school you should go to.
- *An Interdict* – is an order from the court which stops someone from doing something which is against your interests, for example, seeing you or having contact with you.

You may not agree with what your parents asked for or want to put your own ideas forward. If so, the Act says the court can let you ask for one of these orders yourself.

Even if you live with one parent rather than the other, as a result of what the court decides, both your parents will go on having responsibility for you while you are a child.

If you want to know more about this part of the Act, ask a lawyer, the Scottish Child Law Centre, Citizens' Advice Bureau or your local Youth Enquiry Service.

Who can you speak to?

- Your local Youth Enquiry Service.
- Your local Citizens, Advice Bureau.
- Scottish Child Law Centre. Freephone (for under-18s only) (Tel 0800 317500).
- ChildLine (Tel 0800 111) 24-hour freephone service.

All the above organisations will have other leaflets and booklets to help you.

© *Scottish Child Law Centre*
August, 1998

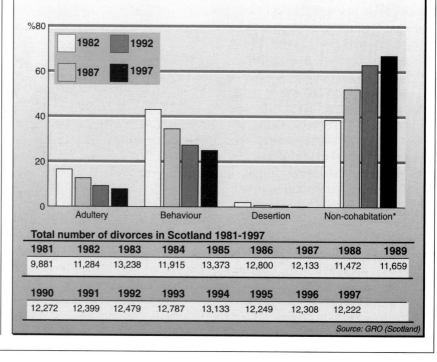

Number of divorces in Scotland

In 1997, non-cohabitation was the most frequent reason for divorce (67 per cent), followed by behaviour (25 per cent) and adultery (7 per cent). Non-cohabitation (both 2 years and consent and 5 years combined) asgrounds for a divorce has increased from 38.5 per cent in 1982 to 67 per cent in 1997; and adultery has fallen from 16.5 per cent in 1982 to 7.8 per cent in 1997.

Total number of divorces in Scotland 1981-1997								
1981	1982	1983	1984	1985	1986	1987	1988	1989
9,881	11,284	13,238	11,915	13,373	12,800	12,133	11,472	11,659
1990	1991	1992	1993	1994	1995	1996	1997	
12,272	12,399	12,479	12,787	13,133	12,249	12,308	12,222	

Source: GRO (Scotland)

What will happen to me if my parents split up or divorce?

Most times when parents split up or divorce it is agreed between them who should look after the children, where they should live and who should keep in touch with them.

Both of them will usually carry on looking after you – even if you don't all live together anymore. Even if you live with one of your parents more than the other, both of them will usually have an equal say in what happens to you. (Example 1)

When a married couple split up they are still legally married, even though they do not live together anymore. In order to legally end the marriage, a court has to give them a divorce

Example 1

My mum and dad got divorced six months ago. They both wanted me to live with them. They asked me what I thought about it but I didn't want to say. Because they couldn't agree, they had to get a court to sort it out. The court gave me a chance to say what I thought as well but I still didn't want to tell. The court decided that I should stay with my mum all week, apart from Saturday nights. On Saturday nights I stay with my dad. I realise that my mum is the best person to look after me, for most of the time. I get on really well with my dad, though. I am worried, that just because I stay with my mum more, he won't have any say in what happens to me, and mum will make all the decisions.

Mark (14)

Just because the court decided that you should live with your mum more than your dad, does not mean that your dad loses all his parental responsibilities and rights. Your dad is allowed and expected to have a say in how you are brought up – both he and your mum will make decisions about you.

Questions about your parents' responsibilities and rights towards you may become very important

Information from the Scottish Child Law Centre

when they cannot agree about who is to look after you, where you should live and who should keep in touch with you.

When they cannot agree, they may ask a court to make that decision.

Your parents should give you a chance to tell them what you think about their arrangements for who you should live with and who should keep in touch with you.

You should not be made to tell them, but they should listen if you want to speak to them about it.

How does a court reach a decision about where I should live and who should keep in touch with me?

Before a court makes a decision it must look at, and think about, three things. These are:

1. You, and what is the best thing for you – you are the first and most important person for a court to think about before making a decision.
2. Whether it is really necessary to make a decision at all. A court will only get involved and make a decision if it is better for you that it does so.
3. What you think about what has been arranged for you.

You should be given a chance to tell the court what you think about the arrangements for you. You do not have to tell the court as it understands that it can be very difficult to talk about your feelings and say what you think sometimes. A court should listen to what you say if you want to tell it. When a court makes its decision about what should happen, it should think about what you have told it.

These decisions, about where you should live and who should keep in touch with you, do not always

have to be thought about when parents split up or divorce – they can be asked about at other times as well.

Can only my mum and dad ask a court to sort out where I should live and who should stay in touch with me?

No – not just your mum and dad can ask a court to sort this out. Other people can do this too. These people are:

1. You

You can ask for a decision to make sure you can stay with, or keep in touch with, the people you want to. (Example 2)

2. Anyone who is close to you like a member of your family or a close family friend can ask a court to do this.

Anyone who is close to you, like your gran, your auntie or your uncle, can ask for a decision to make sure they can have you stay with them or keep in touch with you. (Example 3)

Example 2

My mum and dad got divorced 5 years ago and I live with my dad. My mum has married again and has two wee children – Liam (3) and Rebecca (1). I used to see them a lot. A few months ago I fell out with my mum and she says I am not allowed to see Liam and Rebecca anymore. I am really upset because I get on really well with them. I miss them a lot.

Samantha (13)

If you can't reach an agreement with your mum, you can go to court. You can ask the court whether it thinks you should be allowed to see Liam and Rebecca. If the court does think it would be a good idea for Liam and Rebecca, for you to see them, it will make something called a contact order. A contact order would mean that you are entitled to see Liam and Rebecca.

Example 3

My dad and Louise split up a month ago. They never got married but had been together for ages – since I was about three. Louise isn't really my mum but that doesn't make any difference to the way I feel about her. She is the only mum I've ever known. Since she left, I have been very upset – the problem is dad is really angry and won't let me see her. He says that because she is not my real mum she doesn't have any right to see me – I should just forget about her. That is just too difficult for me to do. I have met Louise a few times after school – dad doesn't know though. I know Louise still wants to see me. Is there anything we can do?

Kerry (14)

Because Louise isn't your real mum, she doesn't have an automatic right to see you. However, if you both want to see each other, there are things that can be done. The first thing to do is to work out if you, your dad and Louise can agree a way for you to see each other. If that doesn't work, then it would be possible for

Louise, as someone who is close to you, to go to court and ask for a contact order. A contact order would mean that Louise would be entitled to keep in touch with you.

Don't forget – it would also be possible for you to go to court to ask for a contact order – this would entitle you to keep in touch with Louise.

These decisions, about where you should live and who should keep in touch with you, will usually last until you are sixteen.

It is important to remember that a court can make decisions about other things which will affect your life, not just where you should live or who should stay in touch with you.

These can be things like:

- Stopping your mum or dad using their parental responsibilities and rights in a way which is not good for you
- Making a decision if your mum or dad cannot agree about how to bring you up – important things like your education or religion
- Giving parental responsibilities and rights to someone else other than your mum and dad, to help that person bring you up

The same people can ask for a court to make these sorts of decisions as well. Remember – these people are: your mum and dad, you, anyone who is close to you.

• The above is an extract from *You Matter*, commissioned and funded by The Scottish Office Home Department and Scottish Courts Administration and produced by the Scottish Child Law Centre.

© Secretary of State for Scotland

What happens to me when my parents split up?

Information for children and teenagers in Northern Ireland

What splitting up means to you

Your parents will always be your mum and dad whatever happens. Parents do not always get on together. Even when they both care a lot for you, they may not be able to live together. Splitting-up and divorce happens quite often now and you will probably know someone whose parents have split up. Try asking them how they got on and what happened to them.

Feelings

You may feel angry, confused or frightened. You might be relieved about some things and sad about others. You may have all of these feelings at the same time which is really confusing. The good news is that feeling bad does not last forever.

Getting help

Talking does help. You may be able to talk to your parents and get some answers to the questions that are bothering you. If your parents find it difficult to discuss what is happening with you, think about a grown-up whom you could talk to . . . maybe a teacher or youth club leader.

Grown-ups don't always find it easy to start talking about important things, but if you ask questions, and let them know you need to talk, they will usually try to help. If you can't find someone to talk to, RelateTeen can provide someone for you to talk to. It is there to help children and teenagers talk about their parents' separation. Call for their RelateTeen leaflet, their telephone number is Belfast (01232) 320709.

Parents' feelings

Your parents will have all sorts of jumbled-up feelings about the split-up. They may be too angry, confused or tired to take time to explain to you what is happening, or to do the usual things with you. They may not understand how you can love your other parent. Things usually get better as time goes on. There are people around who can help your parents sort out their problems.

Deciding where you live

Very often parents can decide between them who is best able to look after you. This does not mean that the other parent doesn't want you, but just that for practical reasons it should be easier for one than the other. Your parents may agree to share looking after you. This may involve you moving between two houses. You may need to be better organised to remember what clothes, etc., you want to bring with you. The bonus is that you can spend lots of time with both your parents.

If you object to an arrangement your parents have made, or are asking a Court to make, you should let them know. If there is a Court case the Court will often ask a Social Worker to speak to you about your feelings and the Court must take these into account. This does not mean that you have to choose who you live with as the Court must take other things into account before deciding what is in your best interests.

Contact with the parent you don't live with

If you mainly live with one parent it may be difficult for you to contact your other parent. You should let the parent you live with, or an adult friend or relative know you want to see them. If the parent you don't live with has moved away you can write or telephone. It is okay to want to have contact with both your parents. Even if they have fallen out they both love you and want what is best for you.

New partners

Sometimes one or both parents may find a new partner. This can make you feel strange because the new partner may seem to be taking the place of your other parent. You may feel angry, jealous and pushed out by the new person or you may like them from the beginning. The grown-ups can also feel awkward at the beginning of a new relationship. Sometimes the parent you live with will get a new partner who may also have children. This may mean getting to know them and perhaps living together as a new family which can be difficult. Talking about how you feel, and finding out the new 'rules' in the home can help to make life easier for everyone.

If the parent you don't live with has a new partner, there is no reason to stop visiting just because there is someone else around.

Some words you will hear

Separation
This is when your parents are living apart.

Divorce
This is when they have asked the Court to legally end their marriage. It doesn't end their relationship with you.

Residence Order
This is when the Court decides who you are going to live with. Residence can be shared which means you live for part of the time with one parent and the rest with the other.

Contact order
This order tells the parent you live with that you must have contact with your other parent or someone else who is important to you.

The Children's Order N.I. 1996

This is the law under which your parents can go to Court if they can't agree on how to look after you while they are living separately. It says your wishes must be taken into account. You can also go to Court to ask them to make or change an order if the Court thinks you are old enough to understand the consequences of what you are asking for. The Court will appoint a Solicitor to represent you. However first you should try to explain to your parents what changes you want and why, as it is easier to change arrangements by agreement than by going to Court.

© The Family Mediation Service N.I. August, 1998

Record 5.3 million people live alone

Record numbers of people are choosing to live alone, research has shown.

About 5.3 million people live on their own in Britain today, representing more than a quarter of all households. This is up from the 18 per cent recorded 20 years ago, and the number is still growing.

Researchers, in their study published yesterday, said the trend had been fuelled by a combination of rising numbers of single and divorced people and the growing proportion, in particular single men and divorced women, staying alone.

The findings follow a two-year study into living trends in the UK

and France, which has experienced a similar leap in the number of lone householders. Dr Ray Hall, who carried out the study with Professor Philip Ogden at Queen Mary and Westfield College, University of London, said: 'Our research shows that more young people are actively choosing to live alone.

'Although one-person households have traditionally been associated with the elderly, there are increasing numbers of people under 40 who are opting to live alone.

'This is especially true amongst professional and managerial classes, possibly because job mobility is important to them.'

The study found that with greater financial independence, more young professionals were buying their own homes rather than renting properties. Although concentrated in urban areas, one-person households were becoming increasingly common everywhere.

Dr Hall said housing markets were already responding to the need to provide homes for smaller, non-family units. The trend away from traditional family structures would also affect other areas of life, including social and welfare provision.

© Telegraph Group Limited, London 1997

Dilemma

Should we divorce, but carry on living together for the sake of our children? By Virginia Ironside

After a terrible Christmas, Dinah and her husband have decided to divorce. But should they stay together for the sake of the children, aged four and five, living separate lives in the same house?

When my parents separated, my mother returned to my father and me every evening and weekend for a year to cook our evening meals. It was all 'for my sake'. All I remember is night after night of awkward silence, or my mother's occasional tragic flirtatious jollity to try to get my father to ask her back. It was utterly mad, totally confusing, and far from being 'civilised' it was downright loopy. I didn't like it. Their unhappy, tortured relationship sat like a fourth guest at the dinner table, killing all spontaneity or joy. Even my mother's delicious suppers tasted of sad dust.

Some new reports say that children would actually prefer their parents to stay together rather than get divorced – but one wonders whether the children interviewed mean that they'd prefer it if their parents didn't get divorced with the proviso that they could live together happily as well. A very different kettle of fish to simply staying together. Living in an atmosphere of strain, deceit, coldness or rows is horrible for children.

Children, feeling they are the centre of the universe, tend to believe, wrongly, that they are responsible for their parents' disagreements, but parents who actually stay together for their sake can start really resenting the children for keeping them trapped in this icy, loveless half-life. Then the children may well blame themselves quite correctly for being part of the cause of their parents' rows. 'We're miserable for your sake,' is the parents' unspoken dialogue, and it's a statement that hangs like a black cloak over children's young lives.

Anyway, are Dinah and her

husband really thinking of staying together for the sake of the children, or is the truth that one or other doesn't really want a divorce and is terrified of being on their own? Or are they both so potty about the children that selfishly they'd rather put their own desires to be close to them first rather than acting in a way that, though shocking and hurtful to start with, may well be the best for the kids in the long run?

Far better for the children is that their parents should part but remain friends or at least on amicable speaking terms, with no backbiting or rows about access, than they should stay together in an atmosphere of hostility.

They might be best off going to

After my parents finally separated they rarely spoke on the phone, used me as a post-box, and only met for lunch once, when my mother was dying of cancer

---

a Relate counsellor, not to try to glue their marriage back together again, but for help in discovering how to part in a friendly way. Certainly, few counsellors would recommend living separate lives in the same house with or without children. What happens when the new young girlfriends arrive, or the old mutual 'harmless' bachelor friend suddenly turns out to be a loving sexy old dog after all? Why should all the old rows not be perpetuated unless the whole place is redesigned with separate entrances and separate kitchens and bathrooms – in which case they might as well be living in separate flats?

After my parents finally separated they rarely spoke on the phone, used me as a post-box, and only met for lunch once, when my mother was dying of cancer. If they could only have got together for my birthdays, or enjoyed the odd drink together when I wasn't there, how much happier I would have been. For a child's desire, second to having parents happily together, is to have parents happily apart. Harmony is what they want and how it's achieved, whether in the same or separate houses, doesn't really matter all that much.

What readers say

Avoid a bad atmosphere

My parents were in exactly the same position that Dinah and her husband now find themselves. They stayed together under the same roof for the sake of myself and my younger sister, but had frequent disputes and often made bitter remarks about each other behind the other's back, sometimes in the presence of my sister and me.

The atmosphere was very unpleasant to grow up in, so my advice to Dinah is to seriously consider whether she and her husband can continue an amicable relationship under the same roof. An unpleasant atmosphere at home can be just as damaging for children as a divorce.

Susan Butterworth, Brighton

Don't hurt the ones you love

My parents stayed together 'for the sake of the children' and finally divorced when I was 20 years old. My advice would be move on with your lives and live apart.

My brother, sister and I grew up in an estranged household, filled with arguments – this gave us huge problems with relationships in later life. In fact my sister and I have both had to have professional counselling to come to terms with the effects our childhood has had on us.

Both of our parents are now happily remarried. Dinah and her soon-to-be ex-husband owe it to themselves to get on with their lives through creating new, separate lives apart from each other. The children will grow up much healthier in spirit.

Name and address withheld

Move out and move on

Under no circumstances would I recommend staying together under the same roof. There would be no opportunities for making a new life.

Children are very 'matter of fact' and would soon get used to a situation where Daddy lives somewhere else, especially if both Dinah and her partner are reasonable about access arrangements.

The stresses and strains that drove them apart would still occur by living under the same roof. What if a new relationship occurred – how would Dinah feel about her ex-

---

My father was an emotional bully who enjoyed making mum feel small. Unbelievably, in their seventies, they are still together, but apart

---

husband getting ready to go on a date or vice versa?

Whilst it all sounds terribly grown up and sophisticated, I would suggest it is a recipe for disaster. Children are far happier with one calm, caring partner, than living together for the sake of them. Move out and move on.

J Marshall, Derby

Scars that last a lifetime

Despite the absolutely terrible dilemma Dinah and her husband must be going through, the idea of living in the same house must be a big no-no! I am grown up, with a wonderful husband and little girl aged 11. Our marriage is very happy, however, my parents' 'marriage' was and still is a nightmare.

My brother and I always knew our parents were different from others. No kisses on the doorstep, kind words or hugs to each other. From our earliest memories, mum and dad lived separate lives in the same house. We (my brother joked) must be the only children who wanted our parents to divorce!

My parents have always been indifferent to each other, only seeking glory in each pot-shot. My father was an emotional bully who enjoyed making mum feel small. Unbelievably, in their seventies, they are still together, but apart.

How sad to live such an affectionless life 'for the children's sake'.

Dinah's children will only feel torn and continually aware of their parents' troubles. Unfortunately, these childish views never leave. My brother and I still try to reason with my parents to at least lead some kind of happy existence. As individuals, each parent will grow and be able to give the children love and attention. Naturally the children want parents to stay together. But, not, I can assure you, 'at any price'.

BB, Norwich

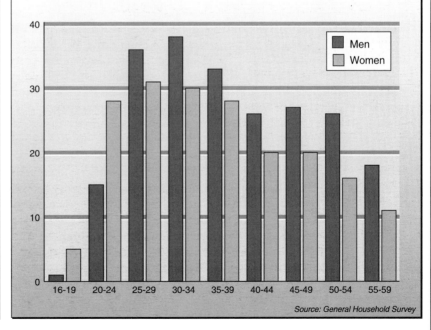

Percentage cohabiting by age and sex

In 1996 22 per cent of non-married men and women aged 16-59 (that is those not currently married and living with their spouse) were cohabiting. Those most likely to be cohabiting were non-married men in their late twenties or early thirties and non-married women in their early twenties to early thirties. Around a third of each of these groups were cohabiting.

Source: General Household Survey

Let children veto divorce, suggests Left-wing report

By Philip Johnston, Home Affairs Editor

Children should be able to veto the divorce of their parents, a report says today.

In a pamphlet for the Demos 'think tank', which has links to Tony Blair, the Oxford don Stein Ringen also says public policy should defend marriage against cohabitation if the decline of the traditional family is to be arrested.

He says the tax system should recognise the common interest in raising the next generation.

He calls for generous child allowances to mitigate the cost of bringing up a family. This would be worth 20 per cent of average disposable family income for the first five years of a child's life, declining after that until the age of 15.

Prof Ringen, a fellow of Green College and Professor of Sociology and Social Policy, says Western societies were 'wrong to see the family as peripheral to modern life'.

'We have yet to understand how rapidly and radically the circumstances of family life are now changing . . . at the cost of economic efficiency and social fairness in our societies,' he says.

While much recent analysis of family decline has come from the political Right, Prof Ringen writes from a liberal perspective.

'I wish to shake my fellow liberals out of their libertarian complacency about the decline of the family,' he writes. He argues that families must be supported against the increasing individualism of modern life.

'Formal marriage should be encouraged and informal cohabitation discouraged,' he says. 'If society is neutral on cohabitation versus marriage, the likelihood is that cohabitation advances over marriage. New unions of weak commitment are encouraged.'

Prof Ringen's concerns are

borne out by statistics predicting that one child in four will experience family breakdown if current divorce rates continue. Over the past 30 years there has also been a rise in the number of cohabiting couples with children and in one-parent families.

The Demos pamphlet, *The Family in Question*, says families need a firm basis in marriage or contract to enable all members, including children, to join in decisions affecting them, notably divorce and abortion.

'Through the acceptance of informal cohabitation, decision making on family formation has been effectively deregulated,' Prof Ringen says. 'The availability of cohabitation encourages unions of weak commitment. Divorce and abortion are increasingly subject to individual decision making.

'In these matters, the libertarian principle of unfettered individualism has crowded out the more demanding and difficult liberal ethic of equal say and joint decision making.'

Prof Ringen also calls for the enfranchisement of children, with voting at 16, and a proxy vote for younger children, exercised by mothers.

This empowerment of children should also be recognised within the family unit, especially when parents are considering divorce. 'Current divorce law and practice give priority to the preference to end a union above a preference to continue it,' he says.

'A child could obviously not enforce divorce against the will of the parents but there might be arguments to suggest that a child's opinion should have some priority if the child is against divorce. If that were accepted, two children in agreement would have a right of veto, even if the parents agreed they wanted a divorce.'

He also believes that the debate about abortion is conducted largely on a 'libertarian fallacy' that negates the importance of community in favour of the individual choice of the prospective mother and avers the absence of rights for the foetus or for the father.

Prof Ringen says the 'standard liberal position' should allow a man opposed to the abortion of his child a say in the matter provided there were no overriding health reasons for a termination.

© Telegraph Group Limited, London 1998

Married parents, a child's best start in life

By Steve Doughty, Social Affairs Correspondent

Marriage is the best way to bring up children, even after parents have split up, researchers have discovered.

Powerful new evidence shows that, even following a divorce, the children of married parents are better off than the offspring of those who simply live together.

It appears to disprove the claims of some experts and politicians who say that cohabitation is simply a 'different kind of family' that is the equal of traditional marriage.

Parents who marry are generally older and more wealthy than those who cohabit, according to the research published yesterday.

Their relationships last longer and when they divorce, almost seven out of ten of their children (69 per cent) remain in contact with both parents. Less than half of the children of cohabiting couples remain in contact with both parents after a break-up (45 per cent).

And just 35 per cent of fathers who have never lived with the mother of their child keep in touch after the relationship is over.

For three years, Mavis Maclean and John Eekelaar of Oxford University studied 249 people who had split up with the parent of their child.

The pioneering study, published in their book, *The Parental Obligation*, shows that a third of fathers who had never lived with the mother paid nothing towards the upkeep of their child. Only one in ten divorced fathers failed to pay for their children.

They found that there was greater bitterness between divorcing couples than between splitting cohabitees, but despite this, divorcees maintained 'significantly better' contact and gave more financial and personal support to their children. The findings run against the belief in much of Whitehall and the academic world that cohabitation should be recognised as the social and legal equal of marriage.

Family law has in recent years given greater financial rights to cohabiting partners while 'no fault' divorce reforms have been accused of stripping marriage of its special status.

Evidence shows that, even following a divorce, the children of married parents are better off than the offspring of those who simply live together

---

A quarter of all women aged between 18 and 49 now cohabit. Statistics show that most cohabitations break up after two years or less. The average length of a marriage is nine years.

Mr Eekelaar said yesterday that this extra time living with the child meant that divorced parents felt more of a sense of obligation to their offspring.

The findings reinforce increasing evidence that children of single parents who never had a full-time partner are far worse off than others.

The report said: 'Children whose parents have never lived together experience a wide variety of family situations: sometimes their fathers are embedded in another family and never have any relationship with the child. Contact with the child is fragile and is usually lost if either parent forms another relationship.'

The study was welcomed by campaigners defending the importance of traditional marriage.

Hugh McKinney, chairman of the Conservative Family Campaign, said: 'This demonstrates there is a chasm that exists between the benefits for children provided by married parents against the problems posed by those who have never been married.

'These findings are not surprising to those who have followed the results of the official neglect of marriage over the last 15 years.'

© *The Daily Mail*
October, 1997

Forget the family says charity . . . we have networks

By Steve Doughty, Social Affairs Correspondent

The ideal of the traditional family headed by married parents has been attacked by the Church of England's leading charity.

The Children's Society preferred to define a family as 'an emotionally supportive network of adults and children, some of whom live together or have lived together'.

Marriage had nothing to do with the reality of family life and no one should discriminate by saying parents should be married, it added.

It called on the Church to rethink its attitude towards marriage and morality so as 'to handle brokenness in human relationships'.

The views of the charity – which has helping vulnerable children as its main concern – put it on collision course with its own president, the Archbishop of Canterbury.

Dr George Carey has repeatedly stressed the importance of marriage, pressing the Government to discourage 'alternative lifestyles' and put marriage at the centre of its social and tax policies.

By contrast, the Children's Society has put forward 11 proposals for the Government – including increased state benefits, more day care for children, and more mediation and counselling for families at risk of breaking down – which makes no mention of the importance of marriage.

Instead, it said: 'The Church, and others concerned with morality and the family, need to take account of changing circumstances and be equipped to deal with changing needs.'

It recommended that the Church 'develop its theology on marriage, family and the community by reflecting honestly on the harsh reality of life for families'.

The society advised: 'It is important, in seeking to define or characterise the family, to recognise the need to avoid discriminating against those whose living arrangements – whether by choice, tradition or necessity – do not match the social norm.'

It said recent developments, including 'significant disagreement and debate about the most appropriate family forms', demanded a rethink of family policy.

> *The challenge is to provide support for families and children which acknowledges changing circumstances*

It dismissed the central role of the traditional, two-married-parent family because 'it is not practicable simply to turn the clock back to some (probably mythical) golden age'.

And it added: 'Certain underlying principles are no doubt timeless, such as parental love, mutual respect and care and nurture of children.

'But the challenge is to provide support for families and children which acknowledges changing circumstances.'

The society rejected any definition of the family referring to marriage as 'too narrow, excluding the extended family as well as other family relationships not represented by marriage or a shared household'. Its idea of the family as a 'network' had shortcomings but did 'resist prescribing or proscribing particular family types or forms', it said.

It added that it was 'important to question' the 'stereotypical' family headed by a husband and wife, saying that 'whilst a particular view of the family may be generally associated with a particular society, it would be unfair to allow policies to reflect only that one dominant view'.

The charity has set out its views in a briefing paper – put together by its social policy unit – distributed to

staff and supporters. The paper makes firm recommendations to the Government on family policy.

The society is one of the leading children's charities in the country and relies on churchgoers for nearly two-thirds of its £26million-a-year income, with £10million coming from taxpayers through the state.

The chairman of the society is the Bishop of Bath and Wells, the Rt Rev James Thompson.

Two years ago he was a key figure in producing a report which said the Church should accept cohabitation and abandon the idea that it amounted to 'living in sin'. The society's views on the family clash heavily with the concerns of the Archbishop of Canterbury.

Dr Carey recently pressed Tony Blair to do more to support marriage, even going so far as to criticise what he described as 'ambiguity at the heart of Government' over the issue.

Lambeth Palace issued a statement making Dr Carey's view plain:

The society's views on the family clash heavily with the concerns of the Archbishop of Canterbury

---

'The Archbishop is anxious to support approaches in Government that will support marriage as opposed to alternative lifestyles.' A senior bishop yesterday underlined Dr Carey's concern at any attempt to push marriage out of policies on the family.

The Bishop of Wakefield, the Rt Rev Nigel McCulloch, who is chairman of the Church of England's communications committee, said: 'I have not seen this Children's Society document but I believe strongly in the traditional viewpoint about marriage.

'I regret very deeply any move away from that as the firm basis for the building of society.'

There was also strong criticism of the charity from outside the Church.

Dr John Campion of the Family Law Action Group described the society's views as 'disgraceful'.

'We need to distinguish between families as they are and the kind of families we wish to encourage,' he said.

'I would have thought the Church would wish to be strong in supporting the traditional family as something we need to see more of.

'We must be sympathetic to families where the husband has died or walked out leaving the wife struggling to keep the family together.

'But that does not mean we should encourage people who choose to become single parents.'

© *The Daily Mail*
May, 1998

Pre-marriage pacts 'a peril' say churchmen

By Gaby Hinsliff

Couples could be coerced into signing pre-nuptial agreements before they marry under proposals to reform divorce laws, it emerged yesterday.

Brides and grooms would be encouraged to wed under a contract setting out how their assets would be divided in the event of a divorce.

Those who declined to sign could end up obliged to split everything 50-50 if the marriage fails, one minister has proposed, as part of the Lord Chancellor Lord Irvine's plans to streamline divorce.

Lawyers warned yesterday that women with children would be the losers if the measure is implemented. Divorce courts traditionally award the home to the wife if she has custody of the children. Clergymen condemned the idea – floated as a way of making couples 'think about

the financial consequences before tying the knot' – for undermining marriage vows.

'The whole point of the commitment to marriage is that it is a real commitment,' said Church of England spokesman the Rev Jonathan Jennings, himself engaged to get married in May.

'If you go into a marriage having planned how it would break up, then I would argue you have not grasped the seriousness of what you are doing.'

Lord Irvine is known to be interested in cutting the legal aid bill generated by lawyers negotiating financial settlements – the most expensive aspect of divorce. His deputy Geoff Hoon has held talks with European counterparts on pre-nuptial agreements. But yesterday, the Lord Chancellor's office distanced itself from the idea, saying

the matter was 'out of its jurisdiction'.

Pre-nuptial agreements have been used in America to dictate everything from what rights a wife or husband has to a partner's fortune, to who will do the ironing.

Family law expert Peter Alexander said pressuring couples to sign agreements would be outrageous. 'You cannot lay down any hard and fast rules,' he added.

'It is always the more powerful person who insists on having a pre-nuptial agreement, a person with wealth is trying to protect it from his or her partner.

'The unfairness of them is really where there are children, or if the marriage lasts a great deal of time, and the circumstances in which they were signed change.'

© *The Daily Mail*
January, 1998

A better way

The benefits of marriage

Research consistently shows that overall, men, women and children fare best within marriage. They are generally healthier, happier and more fulfilled. Despite claims to the contrary, cohabitation is, on the whole, a poor substitute for marriage and an ineffective trial for marriage.

The following presents some of the main findings from the available academic research which compares marriage with cohabitation. Such research is obviously only able to indicate generalities and probabilities but these are a very useful indicator of current trends in society. As one commentator puts it: 'These are indeed only differences in statistical probabilities, but it is such statistical probabilities which shape society.'[1]

Till death us do part: relationship breakdown

- Cohabiting couples are almost six times as likely to split up as those who are married.[2]
- Even where there are children, half of cohabiting couples part within ten years, compared to just one in eight of married parents.[3]

In Sweden, cohabitation is regarded legally and culturally as an accepted alternative to marriage, rather than as a transitional or temporary arrangement. This is reflected in the increasing length of cohabitation and the numbers who never marry at all. But, despite having the appearance of being equivalent, Swedish cohabiting unions and marriages do not have the same durability, with studies showing that cohabiting unions, with one child present, are more than three times more likely to end than marriages.

Even thought the difference is less for younger couples, it nevertheless appears that cohabiting unions are more prone to instability and break-up.[4]

Data in Norway shows that one in ten Norwegian children born to married parents had experienced parental separation by age eight, whereas the same proportion of children of cohabitees had experienced their parents splitting up by the time they were just two and a half.[5]

> ### 'The evidence suggests that unmarried cohabitations which produce children may break up more frequently than marriages which produce children'

Recent research in the UK similarly concludes that 'The evidence suggests that unmarried cohabitations which produce children may break up more frequently than marriages which produce children.'[6]

These figures should not be surprising since it is the premise of

Cohabitation

While some couples may see cohabitation as an alternative to marriage, many decide to cohabit with their future partner before marrying them. Cohabitation prior to first marriage:[1] by age at first marriage and gender, 1995-1997.[2]

| Great Britain | Percentages | |
Age at first marriage	Males	Females
16-19	12	11
20-24	18	21
25-29	34	46
30-34	50	55
35-39	60	59
40-59	44	53
All ages 16 to 59	26	24

1 Those who cohabited with their future partner prior to first marriage as a proportion of all ever married men and women.
2 Combined years: 1995-96 and 1996-97.

Source: General Household Survey, ONS

cohabitation that there is no lifelong commitment to one another and the option of breaking up is consciously preserved. The door is always ajar, so there is always the possibility that one or other will leave through it. Those who view themselves as two individuals sharing a life are going to be more likely to leave the relationship than those who view themselves as two halves of a permanent couple. Thus there will inevitably be more insecurity within cohabitation than in marriage: 'How does the woman know if she will be able to maintain her looks, her attractiveness, her sex appeal sufficiently to keep her partner? He has not made any commitment to her.'[7]

Or, from a different perspective: '...She wants the partner she chooses to share and care and...be emotionally communicative. If he doesn't match up to her requirements, she may very well spin on a heel and walk out of their mutual life.'[8]

A problem often faced by cohabitees who split up is the mixed reaction from friends, neighbours and families. Because cohabitation is, essentially, a private agreement between a couple, those around the couple will understand the nature of the relationship in different ways, and therefore will respond to its dissolution differently.

The following quote, from a man whose partner of five years had just walked out on him, illustrates this problem: 'The worst part of this has been the lack of sympathy. If we'd been married, everyone would have rallied round trying to help.'[9]

Individuals who hope one day to marry (and stay married) should be forewarned of the risks they take in cohabiting as a test run for marriage. The evidence shows that, contrary to popular opinion, cohabitation does not provide an effective trial run for marriage:

- Recent national studies in Canada, Sweden and the United States found that premarital cohabitation increased rather than decreased the risk of marital dissolution.[10]

- Marriages that are preceded by living together are 50% more likely to end than marriages without premarital cohabitation.[11]

'There is convincing evidence that suggests that, rather than strengthening marriage, premarital cohabitation significantly increases the risk of marriage breakdown for both men and women. Moreover, British experience mirrors that of other advanced societies such as the USA, Canada and Sweden.'[12]

Yet, as we mentioned earlier, a widely accepted purpose for cohabitation is as a trial run for marriage. So why should these 'tried and tested' relationships have such a significantly higher marriage failure rate than those whose are 'untested'? The answer probably lies in the more individualistic nature of cohabitation. If the premise on which cohabitation is based is a rejection of the lifelong, public commitment on which marriage is based, temporary cohabitation cannot provide appropriate preparation for the commitment required for a lifelong marriage. Cohabiting couples will continue in ignorance as to what it would really be like to be married because no one is ever able to experience what it means to be married until an exclusive, lifelong, public commitment to the other person has been made. One cannot 'trial run' this lifelong commitment.

'Cohabitors reported lower quality marriages and lower commitment to the institution of marriage, and wives who cohabited had more individualistic views of marriage than those who did not.'[13]

For the procreation of children: raising children

Two researchers in the UK, Buck and Ermisch, analysed the British Household Panel Study in 1995 and were surprised at the relatively high instability of cohabiting unions with children present.[14]

- It is estimated that broken cohabitations are responsible for between a quarter and a half of single-parent families.[15]

In the light of the significantly higher rate of break-up of cohabiting couples and those who cohabited premaritally, even with children, we need to look at the effect of separation and divorce on the children involved. It is not usually the partners who suffer most, but the children, and their suffering can last a lifetime.

There is overwhelming evidence that the break-up of partnerships or marriages is damaging to children; the resulting instability means that children are more likely to suffer from poor performance in school and a lack of concentration, and are more anxious and attention-seeking when young. They are more like to fall ill, to have behavioural problems, to fall prey to solvent, drug and alcohol abuse and to come before the criminal courts.[16, 17, 18, 19]

Recent research also shows that children of divorced parents are more likely to form partnerships via cohabitation, and are more likely to divorce, or to break cohabiting relationships.[20]

Norman Dennis argues that marriage has proven to be a child's best defence against being in a household lower rather than higher in the income scale.[21] A well-known analyst of single parenthood and child support in the USA reported at a seminar in 1997 that she had changed her mind and now admits that marriage is good for children, 'because it strengthened their claim to the economic resources and social capital of both their parents'.[22] Some research has even shown that married men earn, on average, 10% more than otherwise identical unmarried men, including cohabiting men.[23]

The important role of fathers in the raising of their children has frequently been underestimated.[24] In the UK, an unmarried father has no automatic parental rights and responsibilities, other than to give financial support. Rights for cohabiting fathers have to be acquired by a Parental Responsibility Agreement or a Parental Rights Order. A married father, in contrast, has equal rights and responsibilities with his wife over their children.

After a relationship has broken up it has been found that divorcees maintain significantly better contact,

and give more financial and personal support to their children after divorcing, than splitting cohabitees. In the US about 40% of non-resident fathers see their children rarely, if at all, and the longer fathers and children live apart, the less involved fathers become. It was found that after parental separation, children whose parents had not married were twice as likely to lose touch with their fathers as those with divorced fathers.[25]

In the UK research has shown that only 45% of children of cohabiting couples remain in contact with both parents after a break-up, compared with 69% of those whose parents were married.[26] The same researchers also found that more non-resident divorced fathers provided financial support to their former family than was the case for formerly cohabiting non-resident fathers – 68% compared to 31%. This support was also more likely to be given on a regular basis by former married fathers – 44% of formerly married gave regularly compared with just 16% of former cohabitees.[27]

'The evidence seemed to indicate that marriages represented a higher degree of investment in the parental relationship than was the case for … the former cohabitants.'[28]

Absent fatherhood can lead to greater conflict between mothers and their sons: research has found that while teenage girls suffer quietly from the separation of their parents, the aggressive behaviour of boys tends to escalate. Adolescents living with their mother alone reported more frustration and aggression than those with both parents. The research concluded that this is because fathers and mothers fulfil different roles and teenagers are affected when these roles change.[29]

'Children's life chances suffer because of constantly changing homes and an unorthodox type of parenting – whether it is a mother alone or with a succession of partners and stepfathers.'[30]

References:
1. Stand Up For Bastards, Rees-Mogg, *The Times*, 6th March 1997.
2. *British Household Panel Survey*, 1995, Buck, N. and Ermisch, J.,

from the *Guardian* 1st December 1995 and Family Policy Studies Centre Bulletin, 1995.

3. ESRC Research Centre on Micro-social Change, reported in *Daily Mail* 25th June 1997.

4. McRae, op cit., p270.

5. *Family Policy Bulletin*, Family Policy Studies Centre, Winter 1997/98.

6. *The Parental Obligation*, Mavis Maclean & John Eekelar, Hart Publishing, 1997, p137.

7. Together Forever: Marriage or Cohabitation, Searle, D., 1997, unpublished, p2.

8. Are Women Running Out on Marriage? Angela Neustatter, *The Independent*, 23rd November 1997.

9. Quoted from an article in *Elle* magazine, by Anne Applebaum, *Sunday Telegraph*, 23rd November 1997.

10. Cohabitation and Marital Stability: Quality or Commitment? Thomson, E. & Colella, U., *Journal of Marriage and the Family* 54, 1992, p259.

11. This is true for both the UK and USA, for example: The Role of Cohabitation in Declining Rates of Marriage, Bumpass, L., Sweet, J. & Cherlin, A., *Journal of Marriage and the Family* 53 1991, p921, also, Pre-marital Cohabitation and the Probability of Subsequent Divorce, Haskey, J., *Population Trends 68*, 1992, OPCS, and *Social Trends* 24, Central Statistical Office, 1994.

12. McRae, op. cit., p270.

13. Thomson & Colella, op. cit., p266.

14. McRae, op. cit., p270.

15. Reported in the *Daily Mail*, 7th April 1997.

16. *Exeter Family Study*, Cockett and Tripp, Joseph Rowntree, 1994.

17. *Marital Breakdown and The Health of the Nation*, OneplusOne, 1995.

18. *Families and Crime*, NACRO Report (National Association for the Care and Resettlement of Offenders) 1997.

19. Lady Olga Maitland, *Hansard* c245, 28th January 1997.

20. *The Legacy of Parental Divorce: Social, Economic and Demographic Experiences in Adulthood*, Kathleen Kiernan, Centre for the Analysis of Social Exclusion, Case Paper 1, 1997.

21. *The Invention of Permanent Poverty* Norman Dennis, IEA, 1997, p109.

22. Dr Sara McLanahan, quoted at Family Impact Seminar held in June 1997, Washington DC, by Ceridwen Roberts, *Family Policy Bulletin*, Family Policy Studies Centre, Autumn 1997.

23. Male Wages and Living Arrangements: Recent Evidence for Britain, Davies and Peronaci, Birkbeck College, reported in *Bulletinplus*, OneplusOne, Autumn 1997.

24. For example, a 1995 Home Office research study of young criminal offenders found that those who had a bad relationship with either parent were more likely to have offended, and this association was particularly strong for relationships with fathers. The Cambridge Study of Delinquent Development found that having a father who rarely or never joined in the boy's leisure activities at the age of 12 doubled the risk of juvenile conviction. It was also the most important predictor of persistence in offending after the age of 21. Both studies reported in NACRO Report, op cit., p4-5.

25. Fatherhood and Apple Pie, *Family Policy Bulletin*, Family Policy Studies Centre, November 1996.

26. Maclean & Eekelar, op. cit., p 121.

27. Maclean & Eekelar, op. cit., p 127.

28. Maclean & Eekelar, op. cit., p 132.

29. Conflict between Parents and Adolescents: Variation by Family Constitution, Honess T. et al, *British Journal of Developmental Psychology* 1997, p1 and p16.

30. Lady Olga Maitland, *Hansard* c245, 28th January 1997.

• The above is an extract from *For Better or For Worse – Marriage and cohabitation compared*, produced by Care. See page 41 for address details.

© Care

Next generation

Lifestyles for the future

Home alone

The fastest growing category of households will be single people living alone. There are three separate trends at work here:

- The fact that people will live longer means there will be more older people living alone.
- More people will prolong their 'young, free and single' years before settling into committed relationships.
- High divorce rates mean there will be more single-person households, particularly divorced men living alone.

Motherhood: all or nothing

Attitudes towards motherhood will have polarised by 2020. Whereas the baby boomer generation tried to 'have it all' – raising a family and having a career – subsequent generations will choose to pursue one or other path. On the one hand, as many as one in five Generation X women could remain childless. Electing *not* to have children will become an entirely valid option.

'It's not so long ago that "spinster" was a usable term. In the future, there will be lots more electively childless people, and companies will have to market to them as if they are valid people, not as if they are in-waiting to be another sort of person.'
Peter Wallis

'Lots of women will take the "knit your own family" approach. I won't have children, but my closest friend up the road has children and I will undertake to look after them.'
Alex McKie

• The above is an extract from *NeXt Generation – Lifestyles for the Future*, produced by The Henley Centre. See page 41 for address details.

© The Henley Centre

Endless love?

That's what we all hope for when we marry, but a new study forecasts that serial monogamy will soon be all the rage. Maureen Freely is sceptical.

Time: not all that long ago. Place: the nasty end of Kensington. Suze, a thirty-something ad exec, is standing on a corner, trying to hail a cab. She has just attended the single woman's nightmare, a dinner party packed with smug new mothers and their overbearing husbands. Her premature departure had been prompted by one of them remarking that once 'a girl is past her prime, all the best chaps have already been nabbed'. Her retort was: 'What's so great about washing socks and cooking dinner for someone who's just going to lose his hair and spend the rest of his life reading the sports pages?' As she stands in the rain, she promises she will never get married . . .

This scene comes from the opening pages of Penguin's lead title for July, Robyn Sisman's *Perfect Strangers*. It's a comedy of manners in which all ends well, but the reason it is likely to sell well is that it depicts so accurately the nineties working woman's dilemma. There seem to be two and only two choices: either you join the smug brigade or you remain forever single. But according to a report released last week by the Henley Centre for forecasting, it's a problem that's about to become extinct.

By the year 2020, there will no longer be such a thing as a traditional family. Just as no one will expect to have a job for life, so no one will count on a spouse for life. Serial monogamy will be the name of the game. The 10-year marriage contract will have become a reality. The best chaps will get nabbed for a limited time only. We'll drift from new beginning to new beginning in the manner of Zsa Zsa Gabor, Liz Taylor and Jane Seymour.

By the year 2020, there will no longer be such a thing as a traditional family. Just as no one will expect to have a job for life

---

We will suffer fewer domestic tensions, as men will have finally accepted women as equals and will become active parents; we will enjoy more options: instead of living with their blood relations, most people will share households with 'families of choice'. Life will be fluid, flexible, exciting, challenging! The tempo will best suit people born after 1978,

because their upbringing will have equipped them to 'continually adapt to the social change they meet daily'.

Presumably the writers of the report are prepared to do the same. At present all they are doing is extrapolating from current trends, and shaping them into a utopian picture with the help of a few pet think-tank theories. But let's just assume they're more or less right about the future of marriage. Is serial monogamy something we should be happy about? Instead of pontificating in the time-honoured way against feckless divorcees, should the government be accepting it as a reality, even taking steps to support it?

Serial monogamy is not something we have to guess about: a lot of us have been at it for decades. In my not so limited experience, it does not tend to be a deliberate career choice. The very thought that it could be premeditated makes four-times married Jake Hunter splutter with indignation. 'It's not as if I sat down after graduation and said, Mum, I'm going to become a serial monogamist.' What he does admit to is having gone to some lengths during those early marriages to limit the engagement, make sure 'there was always an exit'. He knew that exit would close if he had children,

ANGELA — WILL YOU BE MY FIRST WIFE?

Ken Pyne

and so he didn't have any until his third marriage, at the age of 38.

At the time, he was surrounded by older men who were forever walking out on their families. They acted as if it caused them no pain, and it was only after he had to do it himself that he realised they were lying. 'If there are children involved, it's a serial disaster.' He now has a second child by his current wife, and he sees his first child regularly. 'But I wish I'd started having children earlier. I wish I'd had more. That's the price I've paid for serial monogamy.'

That price is nowhere evident in the future as painted by the Henley Centre. No one even stops to ask what will happen to children in the era of limited engagements, or ask what sort of losses their parents incur after those 10-year contracts have run out. Or even mention the glaringly obvious: that when serial monogamy is the game, the young and the wealthy and the un-encumbered tend to score a lot higher than the ones who are left at home holding the baby. When Mary Corbyn was in her twenties, limited engagements suited her fine. Although her Catholic education had always stressed the sanctity of marriage, her view of her own parents' marriage was that it chained them and kept them from living to the full. In late 1960s London, she found herself surrounded by a lot of other people who agreed that 'monogamy was a dirty word'. All of her serious relationships were open. 'I was a female Casanova.'

She was as good as single when she had her first child: it was much harder than she expected and she changed her ideas about marriage. When a dashing, thrice-married man appeared on the scene and offered to make her his fourth wife, she really did make a commitment. 'And I had so much Catholic guilt about my life of freedom that I did not look very carefully at the track record of the man I was marrying. But the information was there. His exes could have told me. In my arrogance, I thought it would be different for me. Now I think of men like him as retreads. Retreads that need to have regular MOTs.'

It wasn't long before he went off and had another child with another, younger woman. Getting over the humiliation was the easy part. The most gruelling thing about sharing children with a serial monogamist, she says, is that you feel obliged, for your children's sake, to keep in touch with your ex, his other wives and his other children. These reunions are hard to arrange and hard to endure, and although she believes that her son, in particular, needs to have steady access to his father, what sort of message is he getting from this man (who is now with wife number six) about how men should behave?

This, according to Sisman, is the nightmare Suze and Co will face 10 years on, as they slide into their mid-forties: involuntary induction into a serial harem. She has been married once (for 18 years), and intends to stay that way, but when she looks around her, what she sees is a lot of men straying in and out of relationships, and going for younger and younger women every time, their discarded wives left alone with litters of children, struggling to make ends meet with an assortment of insecure jobs.

Her mind boggles at the thought of all the complications this sort of life involves. It's fine if you're young, or very rich with lots of servants to clean up after you, 'but after 45 people get too tired to live that way'. And who would really want to go through the 'whole palaver' of getting to know someone new every 10 years, 'having to suck in your stomach, making sure you've shaved your legs' and for what? If it's for a limited time only, she says, 'you lose all generosity of spirit.

You just want the best deal rather than the open gift. You're not going to pass your heart over the table. You will examine the small print.'

To be fair, the 10-year marriage contract (as proposed by Helen Wilkinson in a Demos pamphlet last year) was only intended for people without children. But life isn't as neat as that. Most of us still do have children. And those of us who end up in serial marriage chains (almost never by intention, almost always by default) have a very hard time bringing them up. There are no winners, just different types of loss.

The ones who stay at home with the children are rewarded with isolation and encroaching poverty. Those who form stepfamilies with similarly afflicted partners can expect a lifetime of managing a family that goes up and down in size like an accordion, of never being able to have the tiniest domestic argument without aggrieved children involving exes who have axes to grind. The ones who move away from all this chaos, and on to bigger, better conquests get the pain of discovering that their children maintain the distance in later life.

There are no policies to support us, and lots that widen the gaps between us. We figure in the public domain mainly as negative examples, as scarecrows to put good married folk off following in our footsteps. Although I am a serial monogamist myself, surrounded by lots of other serial monogamists, I can't find anyone who thinks our beleaguered way of life is a good blueprint for the future.
© *The Guardian*
June, 1998

Family life

- 82% of young women and 78% of young men believe that it is OK for people to live together without getting married.
- 79% of young women and 85% of young men believe that it is a good idea for a couple who intend to marry to live together first.
- 68% of young women disagree with the idea that having children is a reason for parents to stay together even if they don't get along, compared with 51% of men.
- 66% of young women think that one parent can bring up a child as well as two parents, compared with 45% of young men.
- *Young People's Social Attitudes* is available from Barnardo's, tel: 01268-520228, and bookshops, price £18.99 (ISBN 0 902046 30 6).

© *Barnardo's*

Divorcees' pensions 'could hit marriage'

By Gaby Hinsliff, Political Reporter

Plans to give divorcing wives a share of their husband's pension could trigger a decline in traditional marriage, MPs warned yesterday.

Although the move, aimed at protecting women – especially stay-at-home mothers who have no savings – has been widely welcomed, the committee studying it fears a backlash.

The social security select committee said many men would be very angry at losing their nest eggs, and could be discouraged from marrying again.

Veteran Labour MP and former social policy researcher Malcolm Wicks told the special inquiry that if men are put off marriage by the fear of losing assets, women could be left worse off than before.

'We know that in recent years marriage rates have declined,' he said.

'From a man's point of view – the man who has had a divorce and lost a chunk of his pension fund but settles down again with another woman – isn't it likely that this will affect his decision about whether to contemplate a second marriage?

'Given that there are a lot of cohabitations now following divorce, isn't there a chance that your policy has an impact on that kind of behaviour, which could lead to fewer women in future having access to a payment in old age when the second relationship breaks down as they often do?

'If you were that man's accountant or lawyer, what advice would you give him – I think it's obvious.'

Conservative MP Edward Leigh, a barrister and father of six, said there were dangers in making marriage breakdown easier for women. 'People have to realise that when they get divorced, it's going to cost both of them,' he added. 'There will be a lot of pain financially. The trouble is

that many men feel very aggrieved by the divorce process, and the majority of divorces are initiated by women.'

The questions came as the committee took an unprecedented opportunity to pick out potential problems in Social Security Secretary Harriet Harman's plans.

Ministers agreed to the inquiry because they fear a repeat of the Child Support Agency fiasco, in which public credibility was lost once men began to protest at its unfairness.

Labour MP Patricia Hewitt said that under Treasury rules limiting tax breaks on pension savings, men forced to split funds with their wives would be restricted in building their remaining nest eggs back up. Former wives, however, would have greater freedom to boost the share they were given by ploughing it into a new scheme.

Pensions minister John Denham told the inquiry that couples could not be allowed to 'start over' with

tax-free contributions because that would risk making divorce more profitable than staying married.

Labour backbencher Chris Pond feared a repeat of the pensions mis-selling scandal, in which thousands of people were lured out of safe occupational schemes into private pensions providing much smaller returns.

Up to 50,000 women could benefit from pension sharing, which will come into operation in 2000, according to a draft bill published by Miss Harman two weeks ago.

It aims to rescue women from poverty in old age – saving up to £15million paid to them in benefits – and recognise a housewife and mother's unpaid contribution to family finances. Courts can now consider pension funds in a divorce settlement, but there is no mechanism to divide them permanently: ex-wives often lose any rights they had when their former husband dies.

© *The Daily Mail*

I LOOK UPON HIM NOT SO MUCH AS A HUSBAND BUT MORE OF A PENSION FUND

Ken Pyne

The sad fall-out when families split

Divorce rates may be down, but more parents are separating. Four children tell Sue Summers their story

The experts are agreed: when parents divorce, children suffer. And these days, one in four British children will experience the break-up of their parents' marriage before they are 16. For many, it will be the most traumatic event of their lives.

Although the figures in today's government report suggest that the 'upwards trend in the divorce rate could have levelled out', this is because more people are choosing to live together rather than marry. Statistically, such parents are more likely to split up than husbands and wives. A quarter of all children born today are to cohabiting couples, so it is likely that even more young people will at some point have to deal with the break-up of their families.

The views of these children, and of those whose parents divorce, are seldom heard outside the legal system. But next month, in a new BBC2 series, *Children of Divorce*, young people aged between six and 22 will be talking openly about how they were affected.

From these testimonies, and from the children interviewed here by *The Daily Telegraph*, certain common themes emerge: the sadness when children are confronted with the loss of the family unit, and the anger many of them feel towards their parents for not handling the aftermath better.

Recently, Monica Cockett, a research fellow at the University of Exeter, demonstrated how parents can reduce children's post-divorce distress through simple actions. She recommends that the adults present a united front and give the children proper explanations, tell them when and where they will see the other parent again and never expect the children to act as go-betweens.

'There is too much ignorance,' says Mrs Cockett.

'Parents must be given information about the likely effects of their behaviour so that conflict can be avoided for the children's sake.'

She believes that the new Family Law Bill, with its emphasis on promoting mediation rather than allocating blame, should help.

The importance of such efforts cannot be underestimated. Dr Mavis Hetherington of the University of Virginia, world expert on children and divorce, says that for two years after a marriage break-up, all children are disturbed. After that, 70 per cent emerge largely unscathed. But the other 30 per cent suffer complex and long-term effects.

These include disruptive behaviour, low self-esteem, lower levels of educational attainment and poorer economic performance in later life. If the split happened during adolescence, they are also more likely to drop out of school, become unemployed, become sexually active at a younger age, have children out of wedlock and use drugs.

Why some children come through relatively easily while others go off the rails defies simple explanations. Adolescent boys with divorced parents, for instance, tend to do better if there is a stepfather in the house, but girls are more likely to flourish if their mothers do not remarry.

Young children often feel guilty about their parents' divorce, but teenagers can also react badly, feeling their adolescence has been hijacked. Worst off of all are the children whose parents' new relationships break down – they often lose touch with their extended family.

In the light of such evidence, anything that can help children through such difficult times is worth exploring – and listening to their stories is a good place to start.

'I learnt to shut my ears'

Katie is 22 and in her last year at Cambridge. When her parents divorced, she was nine months old, her sister was five and her brother three.

'My father left to live with another woman, and both my parents remarried pretty fast. The hardest time was when my father had another child and it was a girl. I was five: I'd always been the baby and suddenly I'd been supplanted.

'My parents were on terrible terms. Dad never slagged off my mother, but mum really slagged him off. I just learnt to shut my ears to it. I grew up fast.

'I think their divorce was a good thing. I always had two homes which meant that, as a child, I had two houses instead of one – and double Christmas presents.

'I also had the freedom to play one parent off against the other, which is what children in divorces always do because they can. It was a dramatic childhood but a happy one. I always knew my dad loved me.

'When I had a row with mum just before my GCSEs and turned up at dad's place with all my stuff in bags, he just opened his arms and said: "I'm so pleased".

'If he'd told me I couldn't stay, it would have destroyed me.

'My brother had a much harder time. He got chucked out of home by my stepfather. He was made to go and live at dad's and it was catastrophic for him. He ended up turning his back on the family.

'In fact, both my elder siblings had more problems than me. My sister remembers sitting on our parents' bed, but I'd never known them together so I never knew what I'd lost. The first time I saw my parents in the same room was four years ago; it seemed so weird that I had to take a photograph.'

'To me, marriage is a farce'
Flora was 15 when her parents separated four years ago. She is now taking a sociology degree.

'I was always aware of the stress between my parents, and I hated it. Dad had a mega temper and sometimes I was scared. Once, he threw a plate of spinach at the window and the spinach stayed there for years.

'The funny thing is that when they split up, I wasn't prepared at all. I don't think it makes that much difference what age you are. You take your family for granted and it takes a long time to accept that that unit isn't there any more.

'Looking back, I'm not surprised. Dad was very young when they married and mum was ill for years, which was clearly very stressful. But at the time, I didn't realise they were going to separate and I think they could have handled it better. All I had was a call from dad saying he had moved in with someone else, and that was nine days after he moved out.

'It was terrible. I was totally grief-stricken. I was going out with someone who was a twit and the two things together were too much to handle. And my mother was in a really bad way.

'Now, I think it was all for the best. My mum is a stronger person. I've also got a half-brother from my dad and I love that. But I've been thoroughly jealous of him at times because he gets totally different treatment. My dad is much more patient with him. That makes me feel sad because I can see how our relationship could have been.

'My parents' split has also affected the way I feel about relationships. To me, marriage is a farce. My parents were together for 20 years and it ended.'

'I'd still like him to live with us'
Jack, 7, lives with his mother in north London. His parents were divorced last year.

'When my daddy left, he said he'd come back and see me every Saturday, but sometimes he forgets. One day, when he dropped me off, he said that the next weekend he'd take me swimming. He didn't come. Mummy says daddy still loves me, but sometimes I don't believe her. When he takes me out, to McDonald's and a film or to the swings, we have fun. Sometimes we go shopping. Once, he bought me new trainers with lights on but he said to leave them at his flat in case mummy got cross with him for spending too much money.

'Susan lives at his flat. I like her, but sometimes I just want to be with daddy. When he takes me home, I'm sad. I think he's sad, too. Once, he was crying but he just gave me a big hug and went away quickly, so I wouldn't see.

'When daddy takes me home, I'd like him to come inside. But he never does. I'd still like him to live with us. Mummy says it's better now because they were always shouting at each other. Soon we won't even have the same house. Mummy and me are moving to a flat.'

'My parents didn't consider me in the slightest'
Edward was 10 when his parents divorced. Now 42 and a lawyer, he is married with a child of five.

'I was never aware of my parents being happy. When I was about three, I used to hear them screaming at each other and, once, my mother had a black eye. It was no surprise at all when she told me they were going to divorce. When I asked my father if he'd come back to us, he said, "Mind your own business".

'While the divorce was going through they put me into boarding school. The school was a miserable, cold place. I felt completely adrift in the world; I thought my life was over. I also felt guilty, as if the divorce were somehow my fault, and had a complete lack of self-esteem. There seemed nothing worth going on for.

'My mother used to tell me all the dreadful things that my father had done. Each of them was incredibly energetic in undermining the other, and I felt torn apart because I felt loyalty to them both. So I grew up too young.

'I remember worrying about them, particularly my mother, but they didn't consider me in the slightest. Then each of them found new spouses, to each of whom I was of subordinate importance.

'Funnily enough, I didn't blame my parents at the time, or even for years afterwards. But having your own child brings it all into sharp relief. I feel angry for the vulnerable child that I was and determined that the same thing will never happen to my child.

'It's vital that we listen to children when they're caught in the middle of adult relationships. I had no voice.'

Wives 'less happy with married life than men'

By Sandra Barwick

Women are much less happy with marriage than men. Only 56 per cent of wives say they would marry the same spouse again, compared with 71 per cent of husbands, a conference was told yesterday.

Wives were dissatisfied because many husbands had not adapted to the way women's roles had changed. There were too many 'New Women' and 'Old Men', said Penny Mansfield, director of the Government-funded research charity One Plus One.

Satisfaction in marriage, especially among wives, fell sharply after seven years, the charity's conference in London was told.

A Government-funded survey had shown that three out of four men and women agreed marriage and family life suffered because men devoted too much time and energy to their jobs. Ms Mansfield said the unhappiness of wives in marriage had serious implications for husbands and children.

'Research shows that men's physical and mental well-being is closely linked to a stable and supportive relationship with a woman, and that children suffer the fall-outs from parental conflict and broken marriages.'

Most wives helped their husbands' well-being not only by making sure they ate properly but also by fostering their links with family and friends.

The survey found that in the 25 per cent of marriages considered successful, husbands and wives might take traditional roles but both saw marriage as a partnership of values and of power.

Meanwhile, Michael Dobbs, the author whose wife changed her name to O-Sel and became a Buddhist lama, said yesterday that although they lead largely separate lives their marriage is still successful.

Mr Dobbs said he and his wife focused on 'the context of being parents of two great kids' and because of that his marriage had succeeded.

The former Amanda Dobbs teaches at a Buddhist school in Wales and the family farmhouse near Bridport, Dorset, is for sale. She and Mr Dobbs, former deputy chairman of the Conservative Party, have two sons.

Mr Dobbs, 48, said that, contrary to recent reports: 'I am not about to go bankrupt, my family isn't collapsing and I'm not leaving my family to spend more time in politics.'

Speaking on the *Today* programme on Radio 4 yesterday, Mr Dobbs said married men could fulfil their ambitions through being providers. Women bringing up children at home could find personal fulfilment more difficult.

Labour backs prenuptial deals

Couples could be urged to enter prenuptial agreements under the Government Green Paper on the family.

Ministers who drew up the consultation paper say prenuptial agreements should not be limited to pop and film stars in the United States. They could be entered into voluntarily by couples in this country, but the law could be changed to make them binding, removing the discretion of the judge in divorce cases to ignore them.

The aim would be to make couples think more seriously about their responsibilities before they make their wedding vows.

'The agreements can serve a real purpose in bringing couples to face the reality of what can happen if things go wrong,' said one ministerial source.

The Green Paper will also accept that unmarried people can provide a 'loving, stable' home for bringing up children.

The document, to be launched next week, emphasises the importance of rights and responsibilities of couples with children, but carefully avoids passing a moral judgement on unmarried couples.

The Green Paper states: 'The Government strongly supports the institution of marriage while recognising that many couples who choose not to marry provide a loving-stable environment for their children.'

Mr Blair was keen to avoid being dragged into a moral debate about 'back to basics', which exposed the Conservatives under John Major to accusations of hypocrisy when they were hit by a series of sex scandals.

The Prime Minister told the Labour Party conference this month that 'the family is central to our vision of a modern Britain built on the kinds of rights and responsibilities that we learn in the home'.

The Green Paper makes it clear that it is the Government's job to keep couples together for the benefit of their children. Measures to help the family include expanding the roles of health visitors to provide advice to parents, more community support for families, a new strategy to tackle domestic violence, and new powers for registrars to give pre-marriage preparation to couples.

Registrars could be asked to give couples advice before the marriage ceremony, matching the pastoral help provided by clergymen.

15,000 wedding awaydays

More than 15,000 couples took advantage of their right to hold weddings away from a church or register office last year.

The ceremonies were at 'approved premises' – mainly hotels and stately homes. But some couples chose to exchange their vows in far more bizarre surroundings.

They included a cave near Swansea, a Victorian battleship in Portsmouth and London Zoo.

Football grounds – traditionally inundated with requests to scatter the ashes of departed fans on their pitches – are now in the love match business.

Some 4,000 couples took advantage of their new rights in the first year

Among those approved for wedding ceremonies are Old Trafford, Hillsborough, Villa Park and Stamford Bridge.

In the first statistics released since the 1994 Marriage Act allowed weddings in non-traditional locations, the Office for National Statistics said more than 2,000 places have been approved.

Some 4,000 couples took advantage of their new rights in the first year – the number of 'approved' weddings soaring to 15,000 last year. The largest number of marriages in approved premises took place in Kent, where there were 771.

To be approved for marriages rooms must be 'seemly and dignified', open to the public, unconnected with any religion, and no food and drink must be served in the wedding room. Registrars will not allow open air weddings, in tents, aeroplanes, hot air balloons or ships at sea.

The figures showed that in the two years to 1997, the number of religious weddings dropped from 135,000 to 114,000.

© The Daily Mail
March, 1998

Britons delaying nuptial rights as costs top £10,000

Britons are not only marrying older, but the cost of them tying the knot has doubled in the last 10 years, according to survey findings published yesterday.

The average bill for a wedding this year – including everything from an engagement ring to the lacy underwear – is put at £10,151.

So it is perhaps no surprise that people are putting off their special day ever longer, with the average age of marriage having risen by four years since 1988, to 27 for brides and 29 for bridegrooms, according to the survey by *Wedding & Home* magazine.

But it appears romance has not died, even though men are trimming the costs by spending £40 less on the engagement ring. For although 75 per cent of marrying couples already live together, long engagements are still popular – with 96 per cent breaking the news 14 months before.

Wales and East Anglia will be the two cheapest places to get married this year. London remains the most expensive, costing an average £12,707.

The survey also found a growing trend towards the bride and bridegroom paying for their own wedding. Only 53 per cent of parents now foot the bill – 9 per cent fewer than last year. Meanwhile, 6 per cent more couples pay for it all themselves.

However, tradition remains important, with nearly three-quarters deciding to take their vows in church. But of the 2,000 readers interviewed, 5 per cent more than last year had opted to marry in more unusual ways, with bungee jumping, swimming with dolphins or parachuting increasingly popular.

Big parties are also in, with 98 per cent of couples hosting a reception for an average 111 guests. Holding it at home is out, with only 4 per cent risking trashing the carpets.

Eighteen per cent of couples spend £2,275 on a dream two-week honeymoon, with the Caribbean the favourite destination for the second year running. But that is only after the bride has spent £121 on a going away outfit – on top of £742 on her wedding dress.

© The Guardian
March, 1998

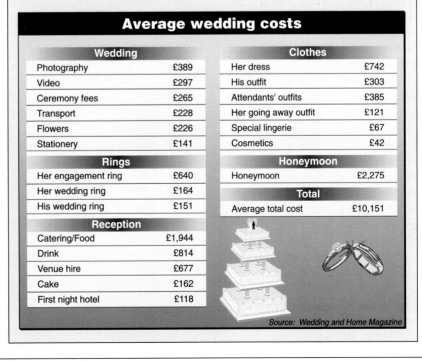

Average wedding costs

Wedding		Clothes	
Photography	£389	Her dress	£742
Video	£297	His outfit	£303
Ceremony fees	£265	Attendants' outfits	£385
Transport	£228	Her going away outfit	£121
Flowers	£226	Special lingerie	£67
Stationery	£141	Cosmetics	£42
Rings		**Honeymoon**	
Her engagement ring	£640	Honeymoon	£2,275
Her wedding ring	£164	**Total**	
His wedding ring	£151	Average total cost	£10,151
Reception			
Catering/Food	£1,944		
Drink	£814		
Venue hire	£677		
Cake	£162		
First night hotel	£118		

Source: Wedding and Home Magazine

Separating or divorcing?

Family Mediation can help

What is Family Mediation?

If you are at the point of separation, or are already separated or divorced, there may be issues causing you concern. These might include parenting issues and the best arrangements for your children, financial matters such as the home and other capital, child support and maintenance, or any other problem particular to your personal circumstances. Family Mediation offers the opportunity to discuss any or all of these matters with a mediator to reach a jointly negotiated settlement.

Family Mediators are impartial and can help you identify the issues, consider the available options and jointly arrive at proposals that will meet your individual needs and those of your children.

What is the Family Mediation Service?

The Family Mediation Service at the Institute of Family Therapy has Mediators who are specialists in children's issues and financial matters. Our professionally and extensively trained team of Mediators includes Family Therapists and Family Lawyers; all are members of the UK College of Family Mediators. We aim to offer the very best in Family Mediation available in Britain at this time.

Will our children be involved in mediation?

If you have children we can help you discuss how to talk with them to ascertain their views and help them to understand what is happening. We will gladly see your children in mediation and will discuss this with you. Children often have different concerns to their parents: it is important for them to be able to express their worries and think about the future. Parents are often better able to reassure their children once they know what is upsetting them.

Is the service confidential?

The service is absolutely confidential. This confidentiality can only be breached if we consider there is a danger of violence or if children are at risk of serious harm.

Do I have to come to mediation?

Mediation is voluntary and nobody can be compelled to take part against his or her will. However, it is often very helpful in enabling people to reach their own negotiated settlement. Our Mediators are specially trained not to take sides; they will help you each to speak and to be heard. They will work to improve communication and reduce levels of conflict.

If you are (or are likely to be) entitled to Legal Aid, you may be required to attend an individual introductory interview prior to mediation commencing so you can find out more about Family Mediation and can decide whether mediation is an appropriate way forward at this point in time.

If you have concerns about taking part in mediation or are worried about meeting with your former partner, perhaps due to violence, harassment or intimidation, please ask to speak to the Family Mediation Service Manager who will ensure your concerns are addressed.

What if I may be eligible for Legal Aid?

The Family Mediation Service is part of the Legal Aid Board Mediation Pilot Project currently being undertaken. If you are receiving Income Support or your income falls below a certain level you may be eligible for Legally Aided Mediation in which case the Legal Aid Board will fund your mediation. The Mediator will be able to let you know if you are eligible at your first appointment.

How much is mediation likely to cost?

The Family Mediation Service is part of the Institute of Family Therapy which is a registered charity. If you are not eligible for Legal Aid, it is necessary for us to seek a contribution based on a sliding scale according to income. Please ask for details. The appropriate fee will be agreed with you at your first appointment.

How long does mediation take?

Mediation usually lasts for between two and six sessions – depending upon the issues you wish to resolve and the degree of complexity. The first session should be considered as an introductory session, during which you can decide whether you think that mediation will assist you, or whether another course of action would be more appropriate.

Will I still need a solicitor?

Throughout the mediation process the Mediator will record your proposals and then summarise them in a Memorandum of Understanding. This is not, at this stage, binding. In mediation you do your own negotiation, removing the need for lengthy solicitor negotiations and legal action. You each still need a solicitor to advise you and, as you may both request, to make any proposals for agreement legally binding. Mediators do not at any time give legal advice.

For further information please contact the Family Mediation Service Manager, The Institute of Family Therapy. See page 41 for contact details.

© Institute of Family Therapy

UK College of Family Mediators

A specialist family mediator may be exactly what you are looking for

Family mediators are trained professionals and have been working in the UK for almost twenty years. They provide impartial help to couples who have already taken the important decision to divorce or separate.

Family mediators respect the couple's decision and help them to make their own sound, mutually agreed and practical plan which will enable both of them to move on with their lives.

They offer two types of service:
- All issues mediation, which deals with a wide range of questions including property, finance and children;
- Children issues mediation, which deals with residence, contact and any other issues concerning children

Family mediators come from a wide variety of relevant backgrounds. A number of established provider organisations are approved by the UK College of Family Mediators which was founded in 1996.

Family mediation works because it . . .

- focuses on dealing with the changes in your life in a constructive way
- provides a safe environment in which you can discuss things
- helps ensure that neither of you is forced or pressured by the other into something you don't want
- encourages communication and discussion about all the issues now troubling you
- helps build up trust for the future
- identifies and explains options for you and your partner to explore.

The time it takes to reach a successful outcome varies and depends on:
- your individual circumstances

- how many issues you have to resolve
- how complex those issues are
- how hard you and your partner are prepared to work.

The UK College of Family Mediators

Promoting best practice – protecting the public
The UK college:
- Sets, promotes, improves and maintains the highest standards of professional conduct and training for those practising family mediation.
- Informs and educates the public about the purpose and outcomes of family mediation and the skills and approaches used by family mediators.
- Makes available the details of registered, qualified family mediators.

The college protects the interests of the public by means of:
- A Code of Professional Practice
- Standards for the selection, training and assessment of family mediators
- A complaints and disciplinary procedure

Finding a family mediator

A number of organisations, approved by the UK College, provide family mediation and related services. All

of them can provide details of family mediators working in your area. Their contact details are as follows:

Family Mediators' Association (FMA)
Offers all issues mediation. Most FMA mediators come from counselling and legal backgrounds and work in pairs or singly. Tel 0171 720 3336.

Family Mediation Scotland (FMS)
Offers all issues mediation and in some locations mediation on children issues only. Tel 0131 220 1610.

Lawgroup UK
Provides training, supervision and continuing professional development, mainly for family lawyers. Mediators work singly or in male/female pairs. Tel 01883 370029

LawWise
Provides mediation training and consultancy for family lawyers together with administrative and developmental support for its trained mediators. Tel 01483 237300.

National Family Mediation (NFM)
Offers all issues mediation and mediation on children issues only. Mediators, who come from a variety of backgrounds, often work in pairs. Also provides training and continuing professional development for mediators. Tel 0171 383 5993.

Solicitors' Family Law Association (SFLA)
An association of solicitors with a code of practice which encourages a conciliatory approach to resolving family disputes. Some members are trained to be solicitor mediators, dealing with all issues. Tel 01689 850227.

The good divorce guide

Divorce with dignity?

According to marital lawyer Helen Garlick separation is a journey: a series of processes rather than a single event. Like any journey, it takes time and planning to reach the right destination intact and with as little stress as possible along the way.

It therefore pays to find out, via books like those written by David Green and Helen Garlick and agencies such as Relate (formerly the Marriage Guidance Council) just what is involved. Because if one thing is certain it is that no-one embarking on getting a divorce has any idea of just how difficult it can all become.

There is only one ground for divorce in England and Wales (Scottish laws vary on many aspects of the divorce process) and that is the irretrievable breakdown of the marriage.

You've got to prove breakdown by one of five facts. Which are:

1. Adultery (but note that it's not just the adultery itself, it's also that you find it intolerable to live with the person that's committed adultery).
2. Unreasonable behaviour. Perhaps alcoholism, or refusal to communicate or poor sexual relations.
3, 4 & 5 all involve a period of separation prior to the divorce.

If you want to start up a divorce petition you have to file a statement of arrangements for the children, a marriage certificate and a fee at a court.

Once the court gets those together it will serve some of the papers on the respondent – who is the other spouse. The respondent then sends the papers back to the court and then you prepare what's called an affidavit in support of your petition – that's saying that all the contents of your petition are true – and from that point on the court should set a date for a decree nisi. Six weeks and one day after the date of the decree nisi you're entitled to

apply for a decree absolute. You don't actually have to go to court in all of this if you don't have any children. It simply goes through on the paperwork. If there are children involved at the date of decree nisi you also have to have a separate hearing which will review the arrangements for the children.

Agony aunts/stress

Although most people have friends who will rally round at a time of crisis and lend a sympathetic ear, it can sometimes be helpful too to talk to a complete stranger – someone who has no preconceived ideas about who is right or wrong. Also, some couples do get 'back together' again; if your friends have spent the last few months supporting you – and saying what a beast he or she is – their embarrassment may make future friendship difficult. The Samaritans are always there to take calls when life seems to be getting on top of us and you will find their telephone number in the book. Alternatively, a number of magazines and newspapers will also respond if you write, summing up the problem. We found

Audrey Slaughter of *She* and Diedre Sanders of *The Sun* particularly helpful. Even if you are in the throes of a divorce, you can still contact Relate (formerly National Marriage Guidance Council). They may not be able to help you mend your marriage but can possibly help you come to terms with the break-up. In some parts of the UK, London especially, the waiting-lists to see Relate counsellors are long, so it makes sense to get in touch with them as soon as possible.

Stress

Obviously splitting up with a partner, perhaps after many years, is an extremely stressful experience. While a degree of stress is not necessarily a bad thing in our lives, most of us have already taken on (through work, family responsibilities etc.) all we can reasonably cope with. The worry and anxiety that usually accompanies a divorce or separation can be just that last straw that breaks the proverbial camel's back. The advice of Dr Peter Tyrer, author of *How to cope with stress*, is that while there is not much you can do to alleviate the

stress caused by divorce and separation, it obviously makes sense to cut back on some of the other stressful areas of life wherever possible. He feels relaxation is vitally important. There are now a number of audio cassettes to help you relax or you might take up yoga – the local town hall or library should be able to give you information about classes. Physical exercise may make you feel very tired but ultimately it too helps your body to relax naturally.

Money

One of the largest costs of a divorce is the cost of the lawyers. According to David Green many people believe that the law contains definite answers to questions such as What are my rights, what are my liabilities? It doesn't. Therefore thousands of pounds can be spent while two lawyers battle it out in court. His advice is to try and work out with each other what it is you want the lawyers to do, how to split the assets etc., what to say about the children. Then tell the lawyers – in writing – what it is that you want them to do.

There are a whole host of things you have to consider – who gets the pension, what about capital gains tax, the 1988 Finance Act changes in the way maintenance is allowable against tax etc. and it is well worth going to an accountant or a Citizens' Advice Bureau before going to the lawyer.

Once divorced you will find that no matter how much – or little – money you now have you will have less. It is therefore vital to find out your rights, especially if you are a single parent requiring maintenance. The sad fact is that almost 2 in 3 women have to chase their ex-husbands over maintenance payments.

There are different remedies open to people trying to get regular payments, one of the most effective is what's called an attachment of earnings order that's made by a magistrates' court directing the employer to pay maintenance directly out of the ex-spouse's pay packet. This of course doesn't solve the problem if someone is unemployed or moves jobs regularly. However, the Government is in the

throes of introducing laws to chase up defaulters more thoroughly.

One answer may be not to even go for maintenance but to opt for a complete and final financial split at the time of the divorce.

Remember – although it may be difficult emotionally to agree guidelines with someone you want to divorce – it is well worth the effort.

Conciliation

Conciliation is not reconciliation. It does not aim to try and repair the marriage but aims primarily to help divorced or separating families when there are problems about custody and access for their children.

Recent research shows that children do best if both parents of the original marriage can manage to develop a good working post-divorce relationship. Satisfactory access and custody arrangements, where agreed to and supported by both parents, mean children are less torn and do better emotionally and at school. Many parents can rebuild a co-parenting relationship after divorce and although this may take time, it is often possible and has benefits for the whole family.

Organisations like the Institute of Family Therapy run Family Conciliation Services. The aim is to help parents agree about the arrangements for their children, rather than the ultimate decision being made by the Court.

It's a confidential service. Couples are usually referred to them by solicitors although people are welcome to approach the service by themselves. Obviously, the service can only help if both parents are willing to go to the sessions (which involve talking through the problems

with a conciliator present) and they prefer to see both parents together for the first session. They will also often like to see the children, either on their own or with the parents.

Couples usually need between four and five sessions with a conciliator discussing the problem before agreement is reached.

You will have to pay for services provided by the Institute of Family Therapy but they're on a sliding scale and based on the income of parents.

Holidays/leisure

In the middle of a divorce probably the last thing anyone thinks about is going on holiday. Yet at a time of great stress it is more important than ever to recharge the batteries – for you and your children. It need not be prohibitively expensive either, but it is important to choose the holiday carefully – the last thing you will probably want (at this particular time) is a romantic hotel, full of starry-eyed couples.

The Holiday Care Service is an organisation that provides information on all types of holidays, including a few you might not have thought of.

They have two factsheets: *Holidays for One-Parent Families* and *Holidays for people on their own.*

Housing

The whole question of who lives where, after a separation or divorce, is so complicated that unless you can come to an amicable agreement (and perhaps even then) you really do need professional advice. The needs of the children are one of the major factors the courts will take into consideration when it comes to dividing up 'the marital home' so who gets to live there, at least until the children are grown up, will depend on who is going to be looking after them. The Citizens' Advice Bureau or local law centre should be able to give you some help.

The Solicitors' Family Law Association, as its name implies, specialises in this sort of work. Their aim is to sort out divorce matters as sensibly and fairly as possible. It is worth remembering that the more work involved in agreeing the terms of a divorce the less money there will be left over – for either party.

If you are a council tenant you should let the council know your new circumstances as soon as possible. This may also involve transferring the property into another name.

Returning to work

For those who have been looking after children full-time for a number of years, the thought of returning to work can be a bit daunting. The local job centre will be able to provide you with details of training – or in some cases retraining – courses. The National Council for One-Parent Families also have a number of training schemes, not so much in specific skills but to give you confidence.

Do get professional advice to help you work out how much better off you will be overall by returning to work. Although your wages or salary will be a welcome addition to the family fortune, some mothers do find that their earnings prevent them from claiming certain benefits and in the long run they are actually worse off. Gingerbread has done extensive research in this area so it is worth getting in touch with them.

Fathers' rights

Many men feel that the law is biased against them. That custody is almost automatically given to the wife – especially if the child is a girl.

It is true that women are more often given custody than men, but it is also true that often the mother is in a better position to look after children.

But this doesn't lessen the feeling amongst many men that they are hard done by.

Families Need Fathers say that both parents have equal rights as well as equal responsibilities. Joint custody, they say, should be the norm, not the exception.

They publish a regular newsletter and hold regular 'Walk-in, Talk-in' sessions at which members and non-members can meet to discuss all matters to do with access, maintenance, custody care and control.

They also sponsor conferences dealing with access and stress that, despite the name, they are open to women as well as men.

The other person

People are often worried about disclosing the name of the other man or woman involved in a divorce that's being pursued on the grounds of adultery.

Yet, as Jill Black points out (*Divorce – The Things You Thought You'd Never Need to Know*: JM Black), this may be because they do not appreciate that nowadays divorces attract virtually no publicity – the days when big suits attracted large crowds to the court and made the headlines in all the papers are gone for good. The reason for this is that most divorces are now granted by a special procedure which means that the names of those involved are unlikely to be mentioned more than once or twice in court in public, and no details of the case are given out at all.

In the majority of cases therefore it would be foolish to be worried about informing the court of the name of the other person involved. If you do know the name you must tell the court in your petition. If, on the other hand, you do not know the name of the other person, the respondent is not prepared to disclose it to you, and you cannot reasonably be expected to find it out, a divorce can be obtained on the basis of adultery with a 'person unknown'.

From the other side – if you are named in a divorce as the co-respondent you have the right to take part in the divorce proceedings in as far as they involve you. The court will provide you with copies of all the relevant divorce papers and you will have the opportunity to confirm or deny anything said about you in the divorce proceedings.

Custody

As we become a more cosmopolitan society, an increasing number of

British nationals form relationships with people from abroad – people they meet through their holidays or their work. While many of them live happily ever after, when something goes wrong – and children are involved – the whole question of who gets custody of the children is far more complicated than in other divorce cases. It is perhaps natural for both sets of parents to want to bring the child up in their own country, but in extreme cases, when the law doesn't seem to be going the way one partner wants, he or she will resort to abduction – the kidnapping of the child from one parent by the other.

REUNITE (National Council for Abducted Children) is an organisation providing practical advice and support to parents and guardians who have had their children abducted, or who fear abduction may occur. It was founded in 1987 by a group of mothers and, as it is run entirely by volunteers at present, it may well take them a while to respond to new enquiries.

If a child is abducted it is important, however, to take action as soon as possible. It is a very trying dilemma because while it can seem to take forever to get any action, the longer the child spends with the 'kidnapping-parent' the less keen the courts become to force the child to return to the original parent – on the grounds it will cause further upset.

What to do

Get the Government on your side.

It is important to register the abduction of your child(ren) with the Lord Chancellor's Office. It is possible they will be able to negotiate with the other country, particularly if it belongs to the Hague Convention.

Some countries have signed an agreement with Britain and the Child Abduction Unit at the Lord Chancellor's Department. They will be able to give you more details. They will also provide you with a form to fill in so do not send in all the details in the first instance.

If you are dealing with a country that has no agreement with Britain, then write to: Foreign and Commonwealth Office Consular Department,

Clive House, Petty France, London, SW1 9HD (tel: 0171 270 3000).

The Lord Chancellor's Office holds a list of solicitors who are experts on child abduction cases. Your solicitor may want to get in touch with them. If you have not appointed a solicitor, it is worth contacting one of them and asking them if they can recommend a solicitor in your area or take on your case themselves.

In some, but by no means all, cases it is possible to get legal aid. For more information on this write to the Legal Aid Board.

Contact your MP – and expect some to be more sympathetic than others.

In addition to offering practical advice REUNITE may be able to put you in touch with another parent in similar circumstances – someone who can share what they have learned with you and offer a bit of comfort and support.

Single again

Being single again takes some getting used to. The pubs and clubs where people meet have often changed since you frequented them – or perhaps you feel they're not for you anymore.

So – how do you go about meeting someone else (if that's what you want)?

A variety of ways. Gingerbread run regular meetings for single parents of both sexes, and organise parties and holidays. If there isn't a Gingerbread group in your area, think about forming one yourself. You'll be pleasantly surprised to find how many other people are in your position.

Taking up a hobby often helps. Anything that brings you into regular contact with other people.

Or there are the dating agencies. Dateline is probably the best known. It currently has over 35,000 members throughout the country.

You join by filling out a detailed questionnaire as to your likes and dislikes and to what kind of person you are looking to meet. You don't have to be looking for a 'serious' relationship – friendship is catered for too. According to Dateline's Frances Pyne a large percentage of the people who sign up with Dateline are divorced and many people, despite rumours to the contrary, do not mind meeting people with children. Some are actively searching for a 'ready-made' family.

The secret is – whatever you do – don't sit at home and mope. Try to live a full life again and put the pain of the divorce behind you.

Useful contacts
- Institute of Family Therapy
24-32 Stephenson Way
London, NW1 2HX
Tel: 0171 391 9150

- The Holiday Care Centre
Second Floor, Imperial Building
Victoria Road
Horsham
Surrey, RH6 7PZ
Tel: 01293 774535

- National Council for One-Parent Families
255 Kentish Town Road
London, NW5 2LX
Tel: 0171 267 1361

- Legal Aid Board
85 Grays Inn Road
London, WC1X 8AA
Tel: 0171 813 1000

- Families Need Fathers
134 Curtain Road
London, EC2A 3AR
Tel: 0171 613 5060

- Solicitors' Family Law Association
PO Box 302
Orpington
Kent, BR6 8QX
Tel: 01689 850 227

- REUNITE (National Council for Abducted Children)
PO Box 4
London, WC1X 3DX
Tel: 0171 404 8337

- The Child Abduction Unit
Lord Chancellor's Department
Trevelyn House
Great Peter Street
London, SW1P 2BY
Tel: 0171 911 7047

- Citizens' Advice Bureau
See your local telephone directory for address details.

- Relate
Herbert Grey College
Little Church Street
Rugby, CV21 3AP
Tel: 01788 573241

© Granada Television

Cohabitation

Cohabitation, by gender, age and marital status, 1995-1997[1]. Among non-married men and women, those in their late twenties and thirties are the most likely to cohabit, although women tend to cohabit at younger ages than men.

Great Britain
Percentages

	Single[2]	Separated	Divorced	Widowed	All non-married
Males					
16-24	9	–	–	0	9
25-34	37	20	50	–	37
35-49	22	22	36	–	27
50-59	7	17	28	7	17
All males aged 16 to 59	20	20	36	10	22
Females					
16-24	18	9	–	0	17
25-34	34	9	35	–	32
35-49	23	9	27	6	22
50-59	9	7	18	5	12
All females aged 16 to 59	23	9	27	6	22

1 Combined years; 1995-96 and 1996-97.
2 Never married

Source: General Household Survey, ONS

The secret of a happy divorce

You've lost the wife, but do you have to lose the children as well? There may be an alternative for weekend fathers

Six years ago, when my partner of 13 years wisely decided that her future lay with someone else, we engaged in negotiations over how the components of our lives should be divided up: I would stay in the house, she would be reimbursed for half the equity; I would keep the television, she would have the fridge. And then there were the children.

There were three of them: an eight-year-old girl and two boys, one aged three and the other 18 months. Neither of us could contemplate life without their everyday presence, and, although I recall arguing that it would be best if they stayed with me in our big, scruffy, east London terraced house, I suppose it was a relief that, from the beginning the children spent three or four days of most weeks with me and the remainder with their mother under the roof of her new companion.

Not having the children around the house every day gave me more of one of the things lone parents treasure most: time. Time to catch up with the shopping, washing and cleaning, time to sit down and think. Mostly, I thought about how to keep paying the joint mortgage on my income alone. Soon I took refuge in the numb survival mentality of what I now call my Gloria Gaynor period.

My great compensation, though, was that I hadn't lost the kids. True, I didn't see them every day. But they were with me for roughly half of every week, so I still took and fetched them from school, nursery and childminder; still cooked for them and ate with them, still read and (poor lambs) sang to them.

In other words, even though the children were no longer daily residents, they remained integral to my daily life, to the ordinary business of ordinary days, in marked contrast to how things might have been had I become a 'weekend parent'. So often such fathers – and, sometimes, mothers – find it difficult to make their children feel anything more than special house guests – whose emotional needs are far harder to meet precisely because they can no longer think of dad's home as being their home too.

> ### Yet I'm convinced that shared parenting has provided my children with the best resolution to their situation that circumstances allowed

I've no doubt that the children feel much the same about my ex-partner's home as they do about mine – it is, without qualification, their home too. Consequently, the three of them – now aged 14, nine and seven – do not see themselves as living in one home, but in two. Without planning it or putting a name to it my ex-partner and I have been practising what is known as 'shared parenting' – a practice which, I believe, can often offer the best way of mitigating the damage done to children by a family breakdown.

'Shared parenting' can be a confusing term. The same two words are often used to describe an intact couple who look after their children scrupulously equally. But, in this context, shared parenting means any post-separation arrangement under which children spend a minimum of about 30 per cent of their time living in the home of each parent.

Things eventually settled into a formal cycle, which still operates today. The children spend alternating stretches of three days in each of their two homes. The six weeks of summer are divided into two blocks so that the children can go on holiday with both parents. Christmas Day is cut in half, the kids waking up in one home in the morning and having Christmas lunch and evening with the other parent. In the event of some special event peculiar to one household falling on a day when the children are scheduled to be in the 'wrong' house, there is enough flexibility in the system to 'borrow' a day on the understanding that it is 'repaid' later.

I don't deny that our system has its drawbacks. Yet I'm convinced that

shared parenting has provided my children with the best resolution to their situation that circumstances allowed.

Of course, they sometimes get tired of shuttling to and fro. Furthermore, managing their needs has been made more difficult by the complete breakdown in relations between their mother and me. The fact that the arrangement seems successful despite this is a strong recommendation for it. The children, I am sure, could not countenance any set-up that relegated either parent to the margins of their lives, something that occurs all too easily with most families that fall apart.

In some places, notably California, shared parenting arrangements are far more common than here and are much more likely to be sanctioned through the courts as a creative alternative to the standard 'residence-plus-contact' formula. American researchers have found that adolescents after divorce who live in shared parenting arrangements scored higher than those not in such arrangements in every category of emotional and psychological development. In their conclusions the researchers stressed that parents should avoid criticising ex-partners in front of the children or doing things that undermined the other partner's importance or authority. Attempts to change children's schools or alter their surnames without prior agreement can be particularly damaging. Yet the researchers also found that the adolescents' sense of belonging to both their parents equally seems to spare them the worst of the wrenching conflicts of loyalty when disagreements are too fundamental to rise above or conceal.

My own experience supports all these findings. However, my greatest difficulty with shared parenting came right at the beginning. Having to broaden my repertoire of parenting skills was tough – but the really difficult thing was lack of money and the anxiety that went with it. For parted parents who run a household on a single income, it is often financially impossible to own a property that is big enough for children to have their own bedrooms.

Notwithstanding such obstacles, shared parenting may be an idea whose time has come. Through it, I have not only gone on loving my three eldest children but gone on knowing them too.

© *The Independent*
October, 1998

The Family Court Service

Working with over 900 parents each year where custody of children is in dispute

The Family Court Service (FCS) works for the Family Courts in cases where parents are disputing arrangements for residence and contact with children.

If possible, the parents are helped to resolve their differences for themselves, through a process of mediation. If this is successful the case needn't go to court, which reduces the emotional stress on the family and saves time for the court.

If the case does come to court, then FCS is there, if required, to represent the interests of the children.

This is not the same as allowing the children to give evidence. Children may be confused, hurt, even blaming themselves for what has happened.

Parents may, without knowing, put pressure on children as part of their fight with each other.

It takes an independent expert to listen to the children, and then decide which solution may suit the needs of the children. It would be impossible to draw these kinds of questions out in the antagonistic forum of the court.

Mediation

As soon as an application is made to the court for a decision on custody of children, an offer of mediation is made. It is up to the parents to accept or refuse – 40% accept. The process is entirely confidential.

Mediation is a service which FCS offer to parents. The aim is to provide a neutral setting where parents, who may even have stopped talking to each other, are given a chance to sort out what they think is best for their children. Mediation involves a meeting, or series of meetings, at which anything relating to the children, apart from financial arrangements, is discussed.

Welfare reports

If the parents cannot agree then the case comes before the court which can then order a report. A court welfare officer then talks to parents and children. The officer may also talk to other relatives, teachers, health visitors and social workers.

The report is given to the court and distributed to all parties in the case. This gives a last opportunity for the parents to settle the matter themselves. If this can't be managed then the court decides, leaning heavily on the report for guidance.

© *1997 Gloucestershire Probation Service*
November, 1998

Welcome to Relate

We hope you will find this information useful. It contains important information about the way we work

What is Relate?

Relate is a national registered charity with over 50 years' experience in helping people with their relationships.

Relate's services

We offer counselling, sexual therapy and other services to help with difficulties in marriage or in any adult couple relationship.

Counselling

We can provide counselling for you and your partner or for you on your own. We can help if you are having problems and want to work them out, or if you want to separate, or if your relationship has ended.

Sexual therapy

Is available for couples or individuals who have specific sexual problems.

Education, training and other services

Many Relate centres also offer education, training and other services for individuals or groups. You can get details of these from your local centre.

Our services are open to anyone who might benefit from them.

We do not offer legal, financial or medical advice. If you need these or other services not offered by Relate, we may be able to suggest an alternative source of help.

What you can expect from Relate

We will offer you your first appointment as quickly as we can, normally within two weeks. If at the end of this appointment it is agreed that Relate counselling or therapy may be helpful, we will discuss at what times you can come on a regular basis, and when this might begin. You can usually come to see us during the day or in the evening.

Counselling sessions are usually once a week for an hour. You will see the same counsellor each week and your counselling will continue for as long as both you and the counsellor feel it is helpful.

Our counsellors are carefully selected and trained by Relate to a nationally recognised standard. They receive continuing support and supervision and have access to a range of professional consultants. In this way we maintain consistently high standards.

Counselling is a private and confidential form of help. This means that we will not give your name or any information about you to anyone outside Relate unless someone's personal safety is at risk. If you would like more information about this, please ask at your local centre.

What we expect from you

We rely on payments from clients to keep our services open to all. We expect you to pay for our services according to your income. The service you receive is not affected by the amount that you pay. At your first meeting, your counsellor will discuss with you how much you can pay for each session.

Once counselling begins, we ask you to make sure you keep your appointments. If you have to cancel an appointment, please let us know as soon as possible, so that we can offer it to someone else. If you miss an appointment or cancel at short notice we may ask you to pay.

We try to provide a caring, effective and efficient service. To help us do this, we invite clients to comment on their experience of Relate. If you want to comment about any part of the service you receive, please contact the manager of your centre as soon as possible. Relate has a written complaints procedure and abides by the Codes of Ethics and Practice of the British Association for Counselling.

Relate will help you whether or not you are married and whatever your age, race, personal beliefs, sexual orientation or social background.

There are over 2,300 Relate counsellors working in 128 centres in England, Wales and Northern Ireland.

Each Relate centre is an independent organisation which is registered as a charity in its own name. All the centres are affiliated to National Relate and abide by its standards.

© Relate

Family mediation

'Separating parents and their children need mediation. It lets us both continue to be parents to our children'

What is family mediation?

Family mediation gives separating and divorcing couples the chance to make their own arrangements for their children's future. Reaching agreement through mediation avoids painful and lengthy court battles.

Who is it for?

Parents whose relationships are over. Partners may separate or divorce but they are parents for life. If you are in this situation, mediation can help you to separate in the best way for your whole family.

How does it help?

Mediators listen to both parents and work with them to reach agreement about which parent the children will live with and when and how they will see the other parent. They can also help you with other questions such as how to tell the children.

Mediation used to be called conciliation, does that mean it has something to do with reconciliation?

No. Mediation is not about helping people to get back together again. Mediators work with couples whose relationships are over. If the possibility of reconciliation arises, you will be encouraged to seek help elsewhere.

How does mediation work?

- You will be offered a meeting with both of you present.
- The meetings are always held on neutral territory. If you want to be seen on your own first, ask and this will be discussed with you.
- Mediators will usually see a couple for two or three sessions. They listen to both sides, pin-point the problems and explore all possible solutions with you.
- Mediators will not take sides in a dispute and they will not make decisions for you.

- The aim is to achieve a practical, workable agreement which is acceptable to everyone.

Do I still need a solicitor?

Mediators do not act as legal advisers. With your permission they will work in co-operation with your solicitor. Agreements reached in mediation are not legally binding but can form the basis of a legal document.

What about the courts?

In Scotland the sheriff dealing with your case can insist that you go to a mediation service to find out more about mediation. If you decide mediation isn't for you, the case will be handed back to the court. In the Court of Session the judge must obtain your agreement before referring you to a mediation service.

In England and Wales mediation is available in most places for those who wish to use it. Some courts have mediation services. There are also other mediation services not attached to the court, which offer you help directly.

When and how do I contact a mediation service?

Come at any stage: before, during or after legal proceedings, usually the earlier the better.

- Telephone or write to a Family Mediation Service, see your phone book for the nearest service. Or contact the national body.
- You can ask for more information before making an appointment.
- You do not have to give your name at this stage.
- Your solicitor or doctor, a social worker, relative or friend could telephone for you as long as they have your permission.

Can I come back later?

As children grow up their needs change and you may wish to alter the arrangements. If at this stage you want the help of the mediation service, you are welcome to come back.

- The above is an extract from *When Parents Split up*, by Family Mediation Scotland.

© Family Mediation Scotland

Getting a divorce

The Family Law Consortium

Getting a divorce nowadays is usually quite straightforward – particularly if a couple agree that the marriage is over. Any difficulties tend to occur more often in sorting out the practical issues such as where to live, arrangements for the children and financial matters.

When concentrating on those related issues, the procedure of actually getting the divorce may seem unnecessarily complicated. The following information outlines the divorce process, highlights key areas and sets out the sort of timetable to be expected.

Who can start divorce proceedings?

Anyone who has been married for over a year provided one of the couple is either domiciled in England or Wales or has been habitually resident here during the preceding 12 months. It does not matter where the couple were married. Admissions of residence and domicile have important tax consequences which we take into account when considering this aspect with clients, and we would liaise with our client's accountant or other financial adviser.

On what grounds can a divorce petition be started?

The only ground for divorce is that the marriage has irretrievably broken down, but there is a complication. A divorce can be granted only if one of five facts, laid down by law as evidence of irretrievable breakdown, is established.

What are the 'facts'?

- A spouse has committed adultery and the other finds it intolerable to continue living with him/her.
- A spouse has behaved in such a way that it would be unreasonable to expect the other to continue living with him/her.
- A spouse has deserted the other for a continuous period of two years or more.

- The spouses have been living separately for two years or more and agree to a divorce.
- The spouses have been living separately for five years or more, whether or not they both consent to a divorce.

If the marriage has 'irretrievably broken down' and one of the 5 facts applies, what happens next?

This will depend on the particular circumstances. It is often a good idea to try and obtain one's spouse's agreement to a divorce at the outset. We may be able to reach agreement with his or her solicitor over the form a petition should take and its contents. For example, if the spouse accepts a petition based on unreasonable behaviour, only a brief and uncontentious outline of the particular behaviour need be given. In an undefended divorce, not saying all that might be said will not generally cause prejudice.

What does the petition actually look like?

Every petition follows the same form. It contains basic information such as names, addresses, date and place of marriage, ages of children and a statement that the marriage has irretrievably broken down. It will also state the 'fact' relied on.

The petition includes a section (known as a 'prayer') which includes a request to the Court for the divorce to be granted. It may include a claim regarding the costs of the divorce itself and list all available types of claims for financial provision. This is quite usual and certainly does not necessarily mean, for example, that the other spouse is seeking all the financial provision that is claimed.

What about the children?

A form is filed at Court with the divorce petition outlining the arrangements proposed for the children. The law encourages couples to try and agree those arrangements.

The form (known as 'a statement of arrangements') is usually completed by the person filing the petition.

Preferably, it should be sent to the other spouse to be agreed before the divorce petition is filed. If agreement is not reached, this does not prevent the divorce from proceeding.

Are financial matters dealt with before the divorce is finalised?

Sometimes. However, often final financial resolution has not been reached by the time the final divorce can be granted. (Any urgent financial problems and temporary maintenance (i.e. financial support) arrangements can be sorted out before a final divorce order is made.) In certain circumstances, it may be advantageous if the making of the final decree absolute of divorce is postponed until all the financial matters have been resolved. This is because the final decree can affect National Insurance contributions, pension and life insurance entitlement, rights under a spouse's Will and protection of rights of occupation in the family home if it is not in joint names. There can also be tax benefits in delaying the final decree until after settlement and implementation of financial matters. We advise about this if it should be relevant.

What happens if a reconciliation is attempted, which later does not work out?

The law specifically encourages couples to attempt a reconciliation even where one of the five 'facts' exists. If the reconciliation does not work out, it may still be able to petition for divorce in reliance on that 'fact'. A maximum six months' reconciliation period is permitted. This can be made up of one six-month period or more than one period totalling up to six months in all. A couple may therefore live together for up to six months after the last act of unreasonable behaviour or after discovery of the last act of adultery and still petition for divorce on these 'facts'.

After separation they can live together for up to six months and still petition, although there must be a total of two or five years apart. For instance, if a couple have a re-conciliation for four months and then agree to a divorce they must have separated at least two years and four months before the presentation of the petition.

Can a petition be withdrawn after it is filed?

It is possible to withdraw or dismiss a petition at any time up to the pronouncement of the decree nisi (the initial decree) with the leave of the Court and/or consent of the spouse if the petition has been served.

Alternatively, a person may decide merely to take no further action in respect of the petition for a short while, particularly if attempting a reconciliation. Once the decree nisi has been pronounced the Court will only stop an application for the decree absolute (the final decree) in exceptional circumstances.

When is it possible to remarry?

A divorce decree is granted in two parts, the decree nisi and, at least six weeks later, the decree absolute. It is only when the decree absolute has been pronounced that the marriage is completely at an end and spouses are each free to remarry.

Religious divorces

In conjunction with a civil divorce, some seek a pronouncement by their religious authorities on their marriage. This may be in the form of a get, an annulment, a talaq or similar. In our experience, the timetable for obtaining them *vis-a-vis* the date of the civil divorce decree is often very important. If this is relevant, we will co-ordinate the civil divorce with other steps being taken for a religious divorce.

Must the divorce take place in England and Wales?

Not necessarily. Although a divorce could take place in England and Wales, in an increasing number of marriages it is possible also for a divorce to go ahead in another

country. It is very important to consider this carefully at the beginning of any separation or divorce. This may apply when the marriage took place abroad, or if one spouse was born abroad, domiciled or resident abroad, has a non-British passport, has property or business interests abroad, or where the children were born abroad or are being educated abroad. A divorce in another county may be more beneficial or detrimental to a spouse, e.g. due to the likely financial provision on divorce. In conjunction with our wide range of international family law contacts, we advise on this aspect.

I have provided for my spouse in my Will. Should I change my Will?

Yes. A result of the decree absolute is that unless one specifically directs in the Will, any provision for a former spouse in a Will or any appointment of that spouse as an executor or trustee takes effect as though the spouse had died at the date of the divorce. This can result in an intestacy or partial intestacy which may not reflect a person's wishes. For this reason a review of one's Will on decree absolute is essential. However, do not wait until then before reviewing one's Will.

Some prefer a short-term Will, to change the provisions of an existing Will but with a view to preparing a more permanent Will after the divorce and when all

financial matters have been dealt with. It is also important to review any nominations under insurance policies and similar arrangements made for a spouse on one's death. This may also include the manner in which the title deeds show the ownership of the family home.

We are able to prepare a Will, at any stage, as well as advising on any estate or other tax planning which could be usefully undertaken at the same time.

Are the divorce proceedings public?

Court proceedings relating to family law are almost entirely dealt with 'in chambers' to which the public and press are not allowed. This is right and proper as such matters should remain entirely confidential and private.

However, the decree nisi is an exception and the press are able to publish its pronouncement. Despite this, the information that they may disclose is limited. In our experience, most newspapers limit themselves to the very bare facts of the divorce. If it is thought the media are likely to take an interest, we can arrange for a short press statement to be issued. However, in our experience this can sometimes increase press interest and so have the opposite effect from that intended.

Timetable

After at least one year of marriage, either spouse may file a divorce petition. He or she is referred to as

39

the 'petitioner'. The petition and statement of arrangements about the children are completed and then lodged at Court, together with the marriage certificate. If the marriage certificate has been lost or a person wishes to keep the original for sentimental or other reasons we can obtain a certified copy. The Court fee for issuing a divorce is £150.

Within a few days of filing the petition at Court either we as solicitors for the petitioner or the Court sends a copy of the petition and statement of arrangements to the other spouse, who is referred to as the 'respondent'. A copy of the petition is also sent to anyone named in an adultery petition. That person is referred to as a 'co-respondent' although it is no longer necessary to name a co-respondent in the petition. If the respondent has instructed solicitors to accept service on his or her behalf the document will be sent to them instead. In certain circumstances, service on the respondent in person (personal service) may be necessary. From the date the documents are received, strict time limits have to be observed by the respondent.

Within 8 days (including day of receipt) of service of the petition, the respondent should file at Court a form called an 'Acknowledgement of Service'. The form asks whether the respondent intends to defend the petition, whether any claim for costs is disputed and whether the proposed arrangements regarding the children are agreed. Although it may have to be signed by the respondent, it is completed by his or her solicitors.

Within 29 days (including the day of receipt) of service of the petition (longer if served abroad), the respondent must file a defence (known as an 'Answer') if he or she intends to defend the divorce. The petition then becomes defended and the procedure set out below does not apply. Defended divorces actually resulting in a final contested hearing are very rare, with a 'compromise' usually being reached. However a delay in the final divorce is inevitable. Defended divorces are also very costly and the final hearing is public and often reported in the

newspapers. Much thought must therefore be given before embarking on this course of action.

Within a few days of receiving the acknowledgement of service from the respondent, and if the petition is not being defended, the oetitioner can apply for the decree nisi (the first stage of the divorce order).

The petitioner swears an affidavit before a solicitor (in another firm), confirming that the contents of the petition are true. Certain other information must also be given, for example whether the couple have lived together since knowledge of the last act of adultery or unreasonable behaviour. Where a period of separation is relied on, the court has to be satisfied that the couple have truly lived separate lives. The affidavit also states if the arrangements for the children are agreed and whether there are any changes to the details filed at the time of the original petition. The affidavit is then filed at the court with an application for the decree nisi under the 'special procedure', the so called 'quickie -divorce'.

If the Acknowledgement of Service is not returned, proof that the respondent has been served is necessary. This may be by personal service or, exceptionally, obtaining a court order dispensing with further service altogether.

When the Court receives the application for the decree nisi, a judge looks through the papers and, if they are in order, gives a certificate for the decree nisi to be granted. A date is fixed for its pronouncement. This is usually about 5 weeks after filing the application at the court. The couple do not have to attend court when the decree nisi is pronounced.

What normally happens about arrangements for the children? If agreement has been reached, the Court is unlikely to interfere. The Court will not make an order regarding children unless it is clear that the making of an order will be better for the child. If agreement has not been reached, the judge may ask the couple to attend a hearing to see what satisfactory arrangements can be made. This may delay the final divorce order.

6 weeks and 1 day after the date

of the decree nisi, the petitioner may apply for the final decree, the decree absolute. The fee is £20. A simple document is filed at court and the decree may be processed as quickly as the next day. But as explained above, there are sometimes advantages in delaying the final decree until all financial issues have been sorted out.

3 months after the petitioner could have first applied for the decree absolute i.e. about 4 months after the decree nisi, the respondent can apply for the decree absolute if the petitioner has not already done so.

The fee is £20. The petitioner can prevent this if it would result in material hardship before a final financial order has been made.

But I thought the law was changing

The Family Law Act 1996 will make a fundamental change to this law and procedure. But it is likely to be another two years or so before it is in force.

Conclusion

The Family Law Consortium hope that this brief guide will be helpful.

Inevitably it is only a summary. If we are not already acting for you and you do not have a solicitor but would like to discuss with us any aspect of this note or your general personal affairs, please E-mail us or telephone us.

We express our thanks to the Solicitors' Family Law Association which has produced a leaflet on which part of this information is based. The SFLA is an association of family law solicitors which encourages a conciliatory and constructive approach to resolving disputes involving families. All solicitors at The Family Law Consortium are members of the SFLA. We actively support its approach and do our best to follow its code of practice, a copy of which we can send to you.

• The above is an extract from The Family Law Consortium's web site which can be found at *www.tflc.co.uk*. See page 41 for address details.

© *The Family Law Consortium*
September, 1997

ADDITIONAL RESOURCES

You might like to contact the following organisations for further information. Due to the increasing cost of postage, many organisations cannot respond to enquiries unless they receive a stamped, addressed envelope.

Barnardo's
Tanners Lane
Barkingside
Ilford
Essex, IG6 1QG
Tel: 0181 550 8822
Fax: 0181 551 6870

Barnardo's (Scotland)
235 Corstorphine Road
Edinburgh, EH12 7AR
Tel: 0131 334 9893

CARE Christian Action Research and Education
53 Romney Street
London, SW1P 3RF
Tel: 0171 233 0455
Fax: 0171 233 0983
A Christian charity which produces a wide range of publications presenting a Christian perspective on moral issues. Ask for their Resources Catalogue.

Family Mediation Scotland
127 Rose Street South Lane
Edinburgh, EH2 4BB
Tel: 0131 220 1610
Fax: 0131 220 6895
Provides mediation for separating and divorcing couples to help them work out agreed decisions on any or all matters.

Family Mediators' Association (FMA)
1 Wyvil Court
Wyvil Road
London, SW8 2TG
Tel: 0171 720 3336
Fax: 0171 7207999
Provides mediation for separating and divorcing couples to help them work out agreed decisions on any or all matters.

The Henley Centre
9 Bridewell Place
London, EC4V 6AY
Tel: 0171 955 1800
Fax: 0171 353 2899
Produced the publication *NeXt Generation – Lifestyles for the Future*.

Institute of Family Therapy
Family Mediation Service
24-32 Stephenson Way
London, NW1 2HX
Tel: 0171 391 9150
Fax: 0171 391 9169

National Council for One-Parent Families
255 Kentish Town Road
London, NW5 2LX
Tel: 0171 267 1361
Fax: 0171 482 4851
The National Council for One-Parent Families has pioneered the development of 'return-to-work' training for lone parents. They produce publications including the recent *Returning to work: a guide for lone parents* (1996) and provide training courses.

Northern Ireland Family Mediation Service
76 Dublin Road
Belfast, BT2 7HP
Tel: 01232 322914
Fax: 01232 315298
Provides mediation for separating and divorcing couples to help them work out agreed decisions on any or all matters.

One-Parent Families Scotland
13 Gayfield Square
Edinburgh, EH1 3NX
Tel: 0131 556 3899 / 4563
Fax: 0131 557 9650

Relate
Herbert Grey College
Little Church Street
Rugby, CV21 3AP
Tel: 01788 573241
Fax: 01788 535007
A national counselling agency for people having difficulty with their personal relationships. The information from Relate in this book is likely to be updated regularly. For an up-to-date list of information and services that Relate provides, please contact them directly at the number above.

Royal College of Psychiatrists
17 Belgrave Square
London, SW1X 8PG
Tel: 0171 235 2351
Fax: 0171 245 1231
Produces an excellent series of free leaflets on various aspects of mental health. Supplied free of charge but a stamped, addressed envelope is required.

Scottish Child Law Centre
Cranston House
108 Argyle Street
Glasgow, G2 8BH
Tel: 0141 226 3434
Fax: 0141 226 3043
Gives advice, information and commentary on child law and children's rights for the benefit of under-18s in Scotland. Freephone for young people (in Scotland) 0800 317 500 (9am-5pm Tues to Friday).
Advice line for adults: 0141 226 3737 (10am-4pm Tuesday to Friday).
Business line: 0141 226 3434 to order publications, get information about training etc. Publishes leaflets, briefing papers, conference papers and other publications, including *You Matter*.

The Family Law Consortium
2 Henrietta Street
Covent Garden
London, WC2E 8PS
Tel: 0171 420 5000
Fax: 0171 420 5005
The Family Law Consortium is committed to working in accordance with the Codes of Practice of the of the Solicitors Family Law Association and the Family Mediators Association and within the ethical guidance of the British Association of Counselling.

UK College of Family Mediators
24-32 Stephenson Way
London, NW1 2HX
Tel: 0171 391 9162
Fax: 0171 391 9165

INDEX

abortion, and rights of the father 14
adolescents
    and absent fathers 19
    effects of divorce on 5-6, 24
age of marriage 27
agony aunts 30

boys, and divorced parents 24, 25

childless people 20
children
    abduction of 33
    of cohabiting couples 15, 18, 19, 24
    of divorcing parents
      contact with non-custodial parents 7, 11, 25
      and custody 32-3, 35
      effects of divorce on 1, 4-7, 24-5
      and the law 40
      in Northern Ireland 10-11
      in Scotland 8, 9-10
      and shared parenting 34-5
      and step-parents/new partners 7, 11
    and Family Mediation 28, 29
    holidays for unaccompanied 32
    of married parents 15
    parents living together for the sake of the children
      12-13
    and serial monogamy 22
    of single parents 15
    vetoing divorce 14
Children (Scotland) Act (1995) 8
Children's Society, and the family 16-17
Church of England, views on marriage and the family
    16-17
cohabitation
    attitudes to 2, 19
    children of cohabiting couples 15, 18, 19, 24
    compared with marriage 14, 18, 18-19
    couples splitting up 15, 18
    and family decline 14
    statistics 13, 15, 18
contact orders 9, 10, 11

dating agencies 33
death, loss of a parent through 5
divorce 2-3, 28-35, 38-40
    acknowledgement of service form 3, 40
    and agony aunts 30
    in another country 39
    attitudes to 1-2, 22
    and custody of the children 32-3
    decree absolute 3, 30, 39, 40
    decree nisi 3, 30, 39, 40
    and the Family Law Act (1996) 40
    and Family Mediation 28-9
    and financial matters 2-3, 17, 31, 38

grounds for 2, 30, 38
and holidays 31-2
and housing 32
naming the co-respondent 32, 40
and pensions 23
petition 3, 38
and pre-nuptial agreements 17
public attitudes to 1, 22
reasons for 2
and reconciliation 37, 38-9
religious divorces 39
and returning to work 32
starting the divorce 3
statistics 7
and stress 30-1
timetable 40
and wills 39
see also children, of divorcing parents

earnings, of married men 19

Family Court Service (FCS) 35
Family Mediation 28-9, 35, 37
family policy
    and the Children's Society 16-17
    and the Government 26
fathers
    absent 19
    rights of 19, 32
    and shared parenting 34-5

girls, and divorced parents 24-5

holidays 31-2
households, one-person 11, 20
housing, and divorce 32

living alone 11, 20

marital breakdown 1-27
    and extra-marital affairs 1, 2
    and premarital cohabitation 19
    see also divorce
marriage
    attitudes to 1-2, 22, 26
    average age of 27
    benefits of 18-19
    children of married parents 15
    Children's Society view on 16-17
    encouragment of 14, 15
    Government policy on 26
    and pre-nuptial agreements 2, 17, 26
    and serial monogamy 21-2
mediation services 28-9, 35, 37
men
    attitudes to marriage 1, 2

and happiness in marriage 26
    pensions and divorcing wives 23
motherhood, attitudes to 20

parents
    divorcing
        and conciliation 31, 37
        and custody 32-3, 35
        and effects on children 1, 4-7, 24-5
        in Northern Ireland 10-11
        responsibilities to children 6
        in Scotland 9-10
        and shared parenting 34-5
    living together for the sake of the children 12-13
pensions, and divorcing wives 23
pre-nuptial agreements 2, 17, 26
public attitudes, to marriage and divorce 1-2, 22, 26

reconciliation 37, 38-9
Relate 1, 30, 36
religious divorces 39
Residence Order 11

Samaritans 30
Scotland, children of divorcing parents in 8, 9-10
separation

and Family Mediation 28-9
    and Relate 30, 36
    see also divorce
serial monogamy 21-2
single parents
    and broken cohabitations 19
    children of 15
single people, after a divorce 33
stress, and divorce 30-1
Sweden, cohabition in 18

weddings
    at 'approved premises' 27
    costs of 27
wills, and divorce 39
women
    attitudes to marriage 1, 2
    cohabiting 15
    and happiness in marriage 26
    pensions and divorcing wives 23
    working mothers 32

young people
    attitudes to marriage and family life 1, 22
    talking about their parents' divorces 24-5
young professionals, living alone 11

Independence Web News

Back	Forward	Home	Reload	Images	Open	Print	Find	Stop

| Live Home Page | Search | Computer | Support | System |

The Internet has been likened to shopping in a supermarket without aisles. The press of a button on a Web browser can bring up thousands of sites but working your way through them to find what you want can involve long and frustrating on-line searches.

And unfortunately many sites contain inaccurate, misleading or heavily biased information. Our researchers have therefore undertaken an extensive analysis to bring you a selection of quality Web site addresses.

★ ★ ★ ★ ★

CareZone
www.dudley-gateway.co.uk
CareZone is a UK based resource for information and help about issues concerning the changing family. If you are worried about your parents' divorce, or if they are worried about you, you need help, information and advice, that's what this web site is for.

Citizens Advice Scotland
www.cas.org.uk
The Citizens Advice Scotland *Guide to Divorce in Scotland* article on this site aims to inform and to give general advice on divorce in Scotland.

Family Mediators Association (FMA)
www.familymediators.co.uk
A wide range of information on family mediation.

BBC Education
www.bbc.co.uk/education/divorce
The Children of Divorce web site is designed to help parents and children who may be dealing with a divorce. Brief but useful.

Relate
www.relate.org.uk/bookshop
This site provides a useful list of their publications on divorce.

ACKNOWLEDGEMENTS

The publisher is grateful for permission to reproduce the following material.

While every care has been taken to trace and acknowledge copyright, the publisher tenders its apology for any accidental infringement or where copyright has proved untraceable. The publisher would be pleased to come to a suitable arrangement in any such case with the rightful owner.

Chapter One: When Marriage Breaks Down

Marriage in crisis, © The Daily Mail, January 1998, *The most important reasons for divorce*, © MORI, *A short guide to divorce in England and Wales*, © Warner Goodman & Streat, *Divorce 'does not damage most children'*, © The Independent, June 1998, *The impact on children and adolescents*, © Royal College of Psychiatrists, August 1998, *Marriage and divorce rates: EU comparison, 1995*, © Eurostat, *When parents split up*, © Family Mediation Scotland, *The Children (Scotland) Act 1995 and you*, © Scottish Child Law Centre, August 1998, *Number of divorces in Scotland*, © GRO (Scotland), Crown copyright is reproduced with the permission of the Controller of Her Majesty's Stationery Office (HMSO), *What will happen to me if my parents split up or divorce?*, © Secretary of State for Scotland, *What happens to me when my parents split up?*, © The Family Mediation Service, N.I., August 1998, *Record 5.3 million people live alone*, © Telegraph Group Limited, London 1998, *Dilemma*, © The Independent, January 1998, *Percentage cohabiting by age*, © Crown Copyright 1998, *Let children veto divorce, suggests Left-wing report*, © Telegraph Group Limited, London 1998, *Married parents, a child's best start in life*, © The Daily Mail, October 1997, *Forget the family says charity . . . we have networks*, © The Daily Mail, May 1998,

Pre-marriage pacts 'a peril' say churchmen, © The Daily Mail, January 1998, *A better way*, © Care, *Cohabitation*, © Crown Copyright 1998, *Next generation*, © The Henley Centre, *Endless love?*, © The Guardian, June 1998, *Family life*, © Barnardo's, *Divorcees' pensions 'could hit marriage'*, © The Daily Mail, *The sad fall-out when families split*, © Telegraph Group Limited, London 1998, *Wives 'less happy with married life than men'*, © Telegraph Group Limited, London 1997, *Labour backs prenuptial deals*, © The Independent, October 1998, *15,000 wedding awaydays*, © The Daily Mail, March 1998, *Britons delaying nuptial rights as costs top £10,000*, © The Guardian, March 1998, *Average wedding costs*, © Wedding and Home Magazine.

Chapter Two: Seeking Help

Separating or divorcing?, © Institute of Family Therapy, *UK College of Family Mediators*, © UK College of Family Mediators, *The good divorce guide*, © Granada Television, *Cohabitation*, © Crown Copyright 1998, *The secret of a happy divorce*, © The Independent, October 1998, *The Family Court Service*, © Gloucestershire Probation Service, *Welcome to Relate*, © Relate, *Family mediation*, © Family Mediation Scotland, *Getting a divorce*, © The Family Law Consortium.

Photographs and illustrations:

Pages 1, 4, 12, 15, 16, 25, 30, 34, 36, 39: Pumpkin House, pages 14, 21, 23: Ken Pyne.

Craig Donnellan
Cambridge
January, 1999